icestars

KEVIN BURSEY

The publishers would like to thank the following sources for their kind permission to reproduce the pictures in this book:

AKG, London/Erich Lessing
Allsport UK Ltd./Shaun Botterill, Clive Brunskill, Graham Chadwick, Phil Cole, Jon Ferrey, Stu Forster, Tom Hauck, Jed Jacobsohn, Robert Laberce, Richard Martin, Gray Mortimore, FredericNebinger, Doug Pensinger, Christian Petit/Vandystadt, Mike Powell, Gary M.Prior, Jamie Squire, Matthew Stockman, Anton want
AP Photo
Colorsport/Iundt-Ruszniewski
Corbis
Hulton Getty
Popperfoto/Joyner, Rjaebye
Topham Picturepoint/Associated Press

Published in the United States by
Triumph Books
601 South LaSalle Street, Suite 500
Chicago, Illinois 60605,
in association with
Carlton Books Limited, 1999

10 9 8 7 6 5 4 3 2 1

Text and design Copyright © Carlton Books Limited 1999

A CIP catalogue record for this book is available from the British Library.

ISBN 1 57243 343 4

Project editor: Martin Corteel
Project art direction: Trevor Newman
Picture research: Lorna Ainger
Production: Sarah Schuman

Printed in Italy.

This book is available in quantity at special discounts for your group or organization.
For further information, contact:
Triumph Books
601 South LaSalle Street, Suite 500
Chicago, Illinois 60605
Tel (312) 939-3330
Fax (312) 663-3557

Captions to pictures in prelims: Page 2 Michelle Kwan;

Page 4 (left) Tara Lipinski, (top right) Michael Weiss,

(below right) Laurent Tobel; Page 5 (top) Marina Anissina &

Gwendal Peizerat, (below) Jayne Torvill & Christopher Dean;

Page 6 Chen Lu; Page 7 Alexei Urmanov.

icestars

KEVIN BURSEY

A celebration of the artistry,
beauty and grace of the
ice-skating world

TRIUMPH

Contents

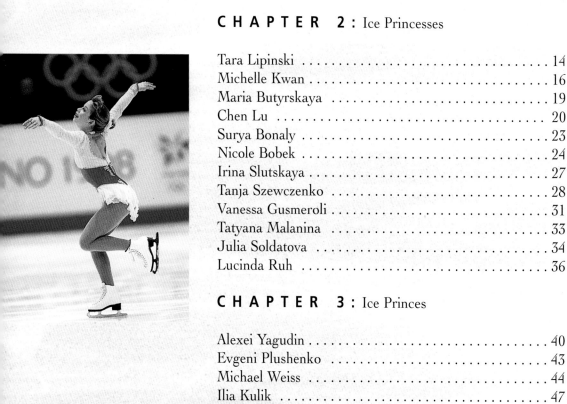

CHAPTER 4 : Great Double Acts

CHAPTER 5 : Stars of the Past

APPENDIX : Ice Champions 110

Introduction

MY FIRST EXPERIENCE WITH SKATING took place when I was eight years old and my mother enrolled me in a local learn-to-skate program. I instantly fell in love with the sport and was inspired and motivated by many of its top athletes during the 1970s and 1980s. Now, some 27 years later, the sport is still a passionate and integral part of my life. I have been fortunate to experience figure skating from various vantage points over the years: competitive skater, professional performer, elite coach and administrator. Through all of these guises, it has been the constant evolution of the sport together with its fascinating personalities that have kept my passion alive.

A sport that has steadfastly stayed in the fast lane of progression, figure skating has developed into one of the high-profile sports of the world. Over the years there has always been the "art over athletics" debate surrounding figure skating. In respect of the music, costuming and glamour of the sport many people have failed to recognize its true physical demands. Today's elite figure skaters must possess the strength of a high jumper, the flexibility of a gymnast, the stamina of a long-distance runner, the balance of a dancer and the mental focus of a top tennis player. Package all these features together with the ability to interpret music through the movement of the body and you have the makings of a world-class skater.

It is the elite skaters that have been responsible for the fast-changing pace of the sport. Each year they return to intense training from May through to September, setting the stage for the following year's competitive season. They are in pursuit of greater physical and technical developments, striving to excel toward greater creative achievement. Following their summer training programs, the autumn brings the start of the ISU Champion Series (known as the ISU Grand Prix prior to 1998) and other international competitions to test the season's new programs. December and January is when most nations host their own national championships which are vital for skaters to earn berths on their country's national team. Late January and early February bring the Champion Series Final, the European Championships and, from 1999, the Four Continents Championships. In an Olympic year the Games will usually fall in February followed by the climax event of the season, the World Championships in late March.

With each year that passes, more feats of athleticism are added to the agenda, further innovations in expression and choreography are made and the demands of becoming a champion are intensified. It is the true champions who captivate and inspire the crowds and move the sport to higher levels of acclaim. It is through those individuals that we lesser people can truly embrace the sport and feel the triumphs and tribulations of our favorite Ice Stars.

1

The History of Figure Skating

The sport of figure skating has evolved into one of the highest-profile sports of the twentieth century, moving from the earliest days, when skating was a means of survival for the dwellers of cold climes, to the glamour and athleticism displayed today. The sport has become ever more challenging for its participants, more appealing for its audience and more accessible to a larger number of people.

Early attempts at ice hockey as depicted in "Winter Landscape" by Pieter Brueghel the Younger (1601).

2000 BC A "blade" made of animal bone, found in the bottom of a Swiss lake and dating back 4,000 years, indicates how people travelled the frozen waters of this time.

1300s AD The Dutch begin making skates out of metal, as opposed to the bone and wooden blades used by their forefathers. Leather belts were used to strap these blades to the user's boots.

1498 The first depiction of an ice skater, a woodcut of Saint Lydwina, the patron saint of skaters, is executed by the Dutch artist Johannes Brugman.

1650 The world's first skating club is established in Scotland, the Edinburgh Skating Club. Members had to be able to skate a complete circle on each foot and jump over three hats.

1750 The British develop the first figure skate, which had a longer, curved blade with a groove. Shortly afterwards, the first skating boot complete with attached blade was produced.

1882 At the first international competition, in Vienna, all participants are required to skate 23 different figures on the ice and perform a four-minute free-skating routine. Norway's Axel Paulsen demonstrates the first one-and-a-half-rotation jump on the ice, the jump being officially named the Axel Paulsen.

1896 The first official World Championships take place in St Petersburg, Russia.

1902 Great Britain's Madge Syers shocks the world by competing in the World Championships at a time when all the competitors were men. She places second, but officials quickly decide to ban women from competing in the championships.

1906 The inaugural Ladies' event is incorporated into the World Championships.

1908 Figure skating is included in the Olympic Games. Pair skating is added to the events at the World Championships.

1924 Figure skating is one of the main attractions at the first Olympic Winter Games. Eleven-year-old Sonja Henie of Norway, who takes eighth place, amazes the world by demonstrating a routine filled with the tried jumps and spins previously performed only by men.

1936 Cecelia Colledge executes the first double jump by a woman – a double salchow – at the World Championships in Berlin. Sonja Henie retires from amateur competition after winning her record 10th world title.

1948 The first double axel is performed by American Dick Button at the Olympic Winter Games in St Moritz.

1952 Dick Button becomes the first skater to execute a successful triple jump – the triple loop – at the Olympic Games in Oslo. Ice dance is included in the World Championships for the first time.

1959 The first triple jump by a woman is landed by Jana Mrazkova of Czechoslovakia at the World Championships in Colorado Springs.

1961 The World Figure Skating Championships are cancelled after a plane crash kills all the American team *en route* to the Championships.

1978 Vern Taylor of Canada lands the first triple axel in history at the World Championships in Ottawa.

1988 At the World Championships in Budapest, Canada's Kurt Browning lands the first quadruple jump – a quadruple toe-loop.

1989 Japan's Midori Ito becomes the first woman ever to land a triple axel in competition at the Paris Worlds.

1990 The World Championships are the last in which compulsory figures are included. Future events would include only the free-skating sections of the short and long programs.

1991 Elvis Stojko becomes the first man to land a quadruple jump in combination with a double jump (a quad toe-loop together with double toe-loop).

1994 American champion Nancy Kerrigan is viciously attacked at the US Nationals, forcing her to withdraw from the event. One of her opponents, Tonya Harding, is said to be associated with the crime and the ensuing media hype increases public interest in the sport to new levels.

1997 At the World Championships in Lausanne, Tara Lipinski becomes the youngest world champion at 15 since Sonja Henie in 1927. Elvis Stojko becomes the first person to land a quadruple toe-loop in combination with a triple toe-loop at the Grand Prix Final in Hamilton.

1998 Tara Lipinski becomes the youngest Olympic Ladies Champion.

1999 At the World Championships in Helsinki, Maria Butyrskaya not only becomes the first Russian woman to win the title but, at 26, she is also the oldest woman in history to do so.

Midori Ito lands the first ever triple axel by a woman.

Tara Lipinski becomes the youngest ever Olympic Ladies' Champion.

Cecilia Colledge who executed the first double jump by a woman.

11

Ice Princesses

They have varied in age. In 1997 we saw the youngest Ladies' World Champion, Tara Lipinski, crowned at the age of 14. One year later she also became the youngest Olympic Ladies' champion in history. Then in 1999, a new record was set. Russia's Maria Butyrskaya became the oldest woman to win the World Championships at 26. Just a few places down in the rankings was Uzbekistan's Tatyana Malinina who had just won the inaugural Four Continents Championships and the Champion Series Final, also at the age of 26.

Regardless of their age, they have become the headliners of their sport and the Ladies' singles is the most-watched event at world championship competition level. So popular with the audience, the Ladies' singles is the final event of the World Championships, allowing for enhanced viewing opportunities.

The mid- to late nineties bore witness to probably some of the finest ladies' skating competitions the world of figure skating has ever known, with a host of teenage sensations, led by the Americans Tara Lipinski and Michelle Kwan. Both girls captivated their audiences with a maturity in presence beyond their years, while still commanding the skill and physical condition to execute all the major triple jumps. Russia emerged as a dominant force in the Ladies' event for the first time in history. There was triumph and despair followed by a final redemption for China's Chen Lu. And we saw several of the premier ladies retire from the eligible rankings to take on new challenges in the professional world.

Each champion has left her mark on the changing face of figure skating. Some will be remembered for achieving new ground in the technical aspects of the sport while others will remain in our memories as true artists. They will continue to enchant their audiences and inspire new generations of skaters to come.

Surya Bonaly (left) and Chen Lu.

Tara Lipinski

TEENAGE SKATING SENSATION

From her first steps on to the ice, it was only eight years until Tara Lipinski became the youngest world champion the sport had ever known.

TARA LIPINSKI'S PASSION FOR WINNING dates back to when she was just two years old; after watching the medal awards of the 1984 Olympic Games on television, she immediately re-enacted the ceremonies in her living room, using an upturned Tupperware bowl as the podium. Who would have thought then that 14 years later this dream of Olympic gold would become a reality?

Tara's career in skating began on roller skates – a sport in which she was a regional champion by the age of five. Once she moved on to the ice a year later, her talent grew at a meteoric rate. At 12 she was the youngest champion of the US Olympic Festival, an event used to profile potential talents for future Olympic Games. The record of being the youngest achiever would follow her career over the ensuing years.

In 1996, Tara competed in her first Senior

World Championships in Edmonton, and although her final placement of 15th was nowhere near the top group, the impression this young 13-year-old made on the Canadian audience and the world's press was the start of what was to become known as "Tara Mania".

The following year, 1997, saw the rise of Tara's true competitive spirit when she defeated the reigning world champion, Michelle Kwan, to become US national champion. Three months later, at the age of 14, she became the youngest world champion since the legendary Sonia Henie in 1927.

In the lead-up to the 1998 Olympic Winter Games in Nagano, Kwan was the favorite to take the title. Many felt that her mature presence on the ice would fend off Lipinski if she skated her program cleanly, and just weeks before the Games began Kwan regained the US title from Lipinski. At the Games, too, Michelle took an early lead in the short program and looked destined for the title. However, she appeared somewhat tentative in the long program, and Tara had the skate of her life to take the gold. Her unmatched jumping abilities, together with her growing maturity and expressiveness, resulted in a performance that many felt was the highlight of the Games. It is something that will live in our memories for many years to come.

Immediately after the Games, Tara decided to pursue a professional career that would allow her more time with her family and studies. Having achieved her dream of

Above: 1999 European Championships.
Right: 1998 Winter Olympics.

becoming an Olympic champion at the tender age of 15, she now wanted to enjoy her success and moved on to professional events and ice show tours, as well as the new challenge of television appearances.

> *"I've always wanted to be a champion, so it was always in the back of my mind. I never told anybody, but I always felt like I was going to do it!"*

Career Record

Personal

BORN: June 10, 1982

HEIGHT: 5ft 1in (155cm)

WEIGHT: 96lb (44kg)

Honors

1995 US Olympic Festival Champion

1997 World Champion

1997 US National Champion

1997 ISU Grand Prix Final Champion

1998 ISU Champion Series Champion

1998 Olympic Champion

POSSESSING A GRACE AND CHARM MATURE beyond her years, Michelle can execute all the demanding technical components of world-class skating with a refined elegance that is uncommon in today's world of athletic figure skating.

At the age of five, she pestered her parents to let her take to the ice with her older brother Ron, who was already playing ice hockey, and her sister Karen, who had just started skating. By the time Michelle was 11, both girls were already competing in the junior level of the US Nationals.

Her early entrance on to the world stage is, of course, attributed mostly to her great

tinctive hair styling and sophisticated make-up. So successful was the transformation that Michelle not only won the US Nationals that season but went on to beat the reigning world champion, Chen Lu, at the World Championships.

Thus 1997 saw Michelle in a defending position as the reigning US and world champion, with her new fellow teammate, Tara Lipinski, eager to challenge her. The added pressure, together with teenage development, seems to have affected Michelle's performances that year and Lipinski took both her titles.

Michelle pursued her Olympic prepara-

A true champion is one who has the heart to rise up after defeat and move forward to win again.

Above: 1998 US Women's Pro Figure Skating.

Right: 1999 World Championships.

UNITED STATES OF AMERICA

Michelle Kwan

THE MAKING OF A TRUE CHAMPION

talent, but also in part to the retirement of Nancy Kerrigan shortly after the 1994 Olympic Games. Michelle was the reserve for the year's world team, and when Kerrigan retired, Michelle was ready to take her place.

She took eighth place at the 1994 World Championships at the age of 13, and created interest the following year when she finished fourth. Many people thought she should have had a medal in 1995, but the judges felt her presence was still somewhat immature for that of a world medalist. So she and her coach, Frank Carroll, decided on an image change.

At the US Nationals of 1996, the audience saw the transformation of Michelle Kwan. Gone were the little-girl dresses and bouncy pony tail, replaced by a more mature-looking Kwan, complete with dis-

tions with a new philosophy, mental toughness and focus, and when she regained her national title from Lipinski just weeks before the 1998 Winter Olympic Games in Nagano, she seemed destined for gold in Japan. Indeed, she was in the lead after the short program, but then a conservative skate in the long cost her the gold – her loss becoming Lipinski's gain.

Michelle spent much of 1999 competing in and winning several of the new Pro-Am events as well as taking her third US national title. However, a bout of flu hindered her performances at the 1999 World Championships, where she placed second to Russia's Maria Butyrskaya.

Having just missed the gold in 1998, Michelle has remained eligible and has stated her interest in taking a second crack at the Olympic title in 2002.

Career Record
Personal

BORN: July 7, 1980

HEIGHT: 5ft 2in (157cm)

WEIGHT: 106lb (48kg)

Honors

1994 World Junior Champion

1996, 1998 and 1999
US National Champion

1996 Grand Prix Final Champion

1996 and 1998 World Champion

"I didn't get into
the skating world just to win
the Olympics or win lots of money.
I really just came into skating to
have fun, to look at it as a sport,
to improve and work hard and see
that hard work pay off."

ICE PRINCESSES

In the wake of immense internal and external doubt, Maria Butyrskaya has proved to the world that perseverance is a major factor of success.

WHEN MARIA BUTYRSKAYA WON THE World Championships in Helsinki on March 27, 1999, at the age of 26, she was the oldest woman in history to do so. The previous four Championships had all been won by teenagers as young as 14.

With her new world title, Maria's competitive history looked impressive. She had won a record six Russian national titles, two consecutive European titles in 1998 and 1999, and had finished just outside the medals at the 1998 Winter Olympic Games.

Yet success came late for Maria, and the road to her world title of 1999 was not easy. She had many years of doubt and insecurity, when her nerves would get the better of her, and at times even her own national federation did not express much confidence in her.

She first stepped on to the ice at the age of four, when her mother enrolled her for lessons because the ice rink was next door to Maria's kindergarten. Before long, Maria began to excel in her newfound activity, was invited to train at the famous ZSKA club, and began to

1999 World Championships.

Maria Butyrskaya

RUSSIA

THE GRANDE DAME OF THE FROZEN STAGE

Career Record

Personal

BORN: June 28, 1972

HEIGHT: 5ft 3in (160cm)

WEIGHT: 106lb (48kg)

Honors

1993, 1995–1999
Russian National Champion

1998 and 1999 European Champion

1999 World Champion

Left: 1999 European Championships.

win competitions in Russia, where she was thought to be a future champion.

During her teenage years, however, Maria grew, went through the normal trials of adolescence, and started to lose interest in her skating. Unable to allow her to continue in their system without her complete commitment, the ZSKA club asked Maria to leave. A brief period of reflection brought her to the conclusion that her love of the sport was too strong and that she wanted to pursue her goals again. So a fresh outlook, together with a new club and coach, started her on the road to success for a second time.

Although she had been winning the Russian title every year since 1993 apart from 1994, Maria did not achieve major international success until, at the age of 25, she won the first of her European titles. Many considered this a one-off performance, but when she went on to recapture the title in January 1999, followed by the defeat of Michelle Kwan in

Helsinki, she had proved that she was a true champion in every meaning of the word.

Maria has stated that she would like to continue competing and to challenge for the 2002 Olympic title. She has finally laid to rest any doubts concerning her ability to perform consistently at the very highest level, regardless of age.

"I have proven to myself and others that physical age does not matter at all in sports."

Her descent from the winners' podium in 1997 was one of the greatest shocks to sadden the world of figure skating. Amid injury and personal turmoil, Chen Lu came back at the 1998 Olympic Winter Games to take her second Olympic medal, proving indeed that she was one of the premier ladies of her sport.

Chen Lu
CHINA

THE FLOWER OF THE ORIENT

Career Record

Personal

BORN: November 24, 1976

HEIGHT: 5ft 4in (163cm)

WEIGHT: 107lb (49kg)

Honors

1990–98 Chinese National Champion

1994 and 1998
Olympic Bronze Medalist

1995 World Champion

1998 Winter Olympics.

ONE OF THE MOST EMOTIONAL MOMENTS IN figure skating took place during the performance of Chen Lu (known in the skating world as Lu or Lulu) at the 1998 Olympic Winter Games in Nagano. Prior to these Games, Lulu had fallen from her world champion ranking of 1995 to an all-time low of 25th at the 1997 World Championships in Lausanne.

Plagued by injuries and coaching problems during the 1996–97 season, she had been requested by her federation to leave her training base in the US and return to China, and as she missed qualification for the final in Lausanne her confidence and spirit appeared gone for ever. However, 11 months later the audience and judges in Nagano were captivated by the performances that resulted in her second Olympic bronze medal for China – and what has been referred to as one of the greatest comebacks in the sport.

Lulu was born in China in the mid-seventies, when there were no indoor ice rink facilities available, and her first ice sessions were conducted on a frozen soccer field, in skates that were hand-made by her father. Being a national ice hockey coach, her father was soon able to secure ice training times for his daughter on one of the newly constructed indoor ice pads.

With a fluidity and grace that set her apart from many of her fellow Chinese skaters, Lulu was considered a complete natural from her very first days on the ice. By the age of nine she was already landing a triple jump, and within a year she was landing all five triples. This was extraordinary in a nation that had yet to make any impact internationally.

At the age of 14 she became the Chinese national champion, a title she retained for nine consecutive years. Her first world medal, which was also the first international medal for China, came in 1992 in Oakland, California. She went on to win four other world medals, including the world title in 1995, and was the bronze medalist in both the 1994 and 1998 Olympic Winter Games.

Chen Lu's success in the sport of figure skating took China to a new level of development within the sport. More ice rink facilities were built and programs were structured to foster the development of other Chinese skaters, enabling China to become a dominant force on the international stage.

Shortly after her last Olympic performance, Lulu turned professional and moved to San Francisco to pursue her career. She enjoys singing and has aspirations to develop her vocal talents. One day she hopes to be able to write and perform her own music, to which she can then perform on the ice.

"I love to perform
and I thrive on the
freedom to express
my emotions on
the ice."

Surya Bonaly

JUMPING DYNAMO EXTRAORDINAIRE

Her early involvement and abilities as a tumbler provided Surya with the founding skills that enabled her to become one of figure skating's greatest female jumpers of the early nineties.

Jumper supreme.

SURYA BONALY IS ONLY THE SECOND BLACK figure skater to achieve international acclaim, after the African-American Debi Thomas, who was the 1986 world champion.

From her first European Championships in 1989, through to her final eligible event at the 1998 Olympic Winter Games, Surya's career has been highlighted by controversy. At the Games, she left her final mark in the amateur field by performing the illegal back-flip in her long program of the competition, maintaining her record of being different and not always conforming to the normal practices of the sport.

Surya was born in northern Africa and adopted by a white French missionary couple. Despite having no background in ice skating, her mother Suzanne became her chief coach in the later years of her amateur career, creating colorful stories to keep her daughter in the headlines.

Initially, Surya's sporting endeavors were in gymnastics, where she was a superb tumbler, developing skills that enhanced her jumping technique once she committed to figure skating. She is one of the formidable lady jumpers of her time, even attempting quadruple jumps at a time when they were just starting to emerge in the men's event.

Although Surya's style and basic skating skills have been criticized, her excellent jumping ability brought her nine national and five European titles – not to mention her three silver world medals and wins at other international events. Some believe that her lack of artistic flair was the reason she lost the 1994 world title to Japan's Yuka Sato. At these Championships, Surya was so disappointed to miss the gold that she initially refused to take her place on the medal podium, and when her medal was finally placed over her head she defiantly removed it.

Surya's amateur days will be best remembered for some of the idiosyncrasies that added color to her performances: her long, thick hair – initially never cut and worn tied back in a double braid to keep it from knocking her out; performing with bare legs, as opposed to the customary tights worn by other competitors; refusing her medal in 1994; and finally for having the strength to rise above the many critics who claimed she was not the overall packaged skater, even while she was surpassing many of her counterparts in the battle to land the triple jumps.

Today Surya is enjoying the professional circuit of shows and events. She relishes the opportunities to experiment with her skating without having to conform to the international skating regulations of the amateur world.

Career Record

Personal

BORN: December 15, 1973

HEIGHT: 5ft 4in (164cm)

WEIGHT: 118lb (54kg)

Honors

1988-96 French National Champion

1991 World Junior Champion

1991–95 European Champion

1993–95 World Silver Medalist

Left: 1998 Winter Olympics.

She had the strength to rise above her critics who claimed she was not the overall packaged skater.

23

Nicole Bobek

MEETING WITH TRIUMPH AND TRAGEDY

The dramas of her career have kept Nicole Bobek in the media's headlines on the occasions when her skating did not. Her sheer courage has proved she can face any demons that may cross her path.

ONE OF THE TOP FEMALE SKATERS IN THE world, Nicole Bobek is also one of the most inconsistent. Her trademark spirals, formidable flexibility, innate ability to interpret music, and her great athleticism in jumping are the ingredients of a true figure skating champion. Yet ever since her first Novice Nationals in 1989, where she won the silver medal, her career has been a roller-coaster ride of controversy, injury and coaching changes.

Bobek has a family tradition of figure skating, for both her mother and grandmother were figure skaters back in their native Czech Republic. Nicole's most successful year was the 1995 season when she won the US National title, beating the favorite, Michelle Kwan, and followed with the bronze medal at the World Championships in Birmingham, England. Her coach at that time was Richard Callaghan, who success-

fully transformed the wild child into a much more committed and disciplined athlete, but their progress was halted when she moved on to what would be her ninth coach in almost as many years.

Although her world medal in 1995 had established her as one of the leading ladies of figure skating, Nicole was unable to capitalize on this ranking when an ankle injury just prior to the US Nationals of 1996 kept her out of the team. True to her vow to return to top form for 1997, she won the bronze medal that year, gaining a place on the 1997 US world team.

Then tragedy struck the day before the Ladies' event of the World Championships in Lausanne. Carlo Fassi, the renowned coach who had pulled Nicole up from her setback in 1996, died of a heart attack the day before Nicole was to take the ice in the short program competition. Ever the fighter, Nicole carried on and skated in memory of Carlo the next day. Although she did not earn a place in the top 10 that year, her courage and strength showed she was not just your average young lady.

She took the bronze medal again at the Nationals, earning herself a coveted place on the American Olympic team for Nagano, where she had to settle for 17th place. Then abdominal surgery to remove scar tissue took Nicole out of the 1999 US Nationals and kept her out of action until late February. This setback was especially devastating for Nicole as she had trained vigor-

Above: 1995 World Championships.

Right: 1995 World Championships.

ously for these Championships and had even rejoined her former coach, Richard Callaghan.

Despite other distractions, she has remained eligible at this time and may well turn up at the 2000 US Nationals in an attempt to reclaim the title she held in 1995.

"Figure skaters have to be perfect little ladies all the time."

Career Record

Personal

BORN: August 23, 1977

HEIGHT: 5ft 5in (165cm)

WEIGHT: 120lb (54kg)

Honors

1991 US Olympic Festival Champion

1995 US National Champion

1995 World Bronze Medalist

ICE PRINCESSES

Irina Slutskaya burst on to the international scene with an energy and an exuberant personality that the world had never seen in a Russian lady. She was a pioneer in changing the perceptions the world had of her homeland.

Irina Slutskaya

CHANGING THE FACE OF RUSSIAN LADIES FIGURE SKATING

ALTHOUGH RUSSIA HAS BEEN DOMINANT IN all the other disciplines of figure skating, before Irina Slutskaya came on the scene, their Ladies' singles skaters had brought a very classical and stoic presence to their performances. When this fresh and exuberant young girl emerged on to the world scene, she brought with her a personality and energy that the skating world was not accustomed to in a Russian Ladies' singles skater.

She began skating at the age of four in her hometown of Moscow, in an attempt to keep at bay the string of colds and viruses from which she suffered. Her enthusiasm and verve overcame any early lack of natural talent, and by the time she was 14 she had established herself as a junior, taking the bronze medal at the 1994

1998 World Championships.

World Junior Championships.

It was at her first senior World Championships in 1995 that Irina changed the face of Russian Ladies' singles skating and endeared herself to the British audience in Birmingham, where she took seventh place. She went on to make history at the 1996 European Championships by becoming the first Russian woman to win the title, following this two months later with the bronze medal at the World Championships.

The Russian federation decided that Irina's image and styling should be made to look more mature for the 1997 season, but the subsequent styling changes, together with the effects of normal teenage development, were not a success. She had to settle for fourth place at the 1997 World Championships, although she was able to retain her European title for a second year.

Wanting to secure a place on the 1998 Olympic team, Irina and her coach went back to what was both successful and comfortable for her to skate to. Still struggling to cope with the weight changes in her body, she lost her European title to teammate Maria Butyrskaya at the 1998 Championships, and at the Olympic Games she finished fifth after a strong free program. It wasn't until the World Championships that she returned to her former confident self and took the silver medal in Minneapolis.

The Russian federation now has a wealth of up-and-coming women to choose from for its world team, and Slutskaya's performance in the Russian nationals for 1999, together with a performance below expectations at the ISU Champion Series Final, left her

without a place in the world team this time.

She has remained eligible and will be returning in 2000 to try to recapture her successes of the past. Despite offers to train in the United States, she has stayed in Russia with her coach and family.

"I like jumps . . .
I love to feel like I
am skating, to feel like
I can really use
these blades."

Career Record

Personal

BORN: February 19, 1979

HEIGHT: 5ft 4in (163cm)

WEIGHT: 114lb (52kg)

Honors

1996 and 1997 European Champion
1998 World Silver Medalist
1998 Olympic Winter Games – 5th

Left: Women's freestyle during the 1998 World Championships.

Tanja Szewczenko

GERMANY

THE COMEBACK GIRL

Tanja Szewczenko took the 1997 world bronze medal at the age of 16. Her dream of furthering this success and taking the title has been hampered by serious health problems and injury, and although she came back with a vengeance in late 1997, health problems again held her back.

Above: 1998 Winter Olympics.

Right: 1995 World Championships

IN A CAREER THAT HAS BEEN PLAGUED BY injury and illness, Tanja Szewczenko has managed to establish herself as one of the leading women of her chosen sport. Her best performance result was at the 1994 World Championships in Chiba, Japan, where she took the bronze medal. Appearing in her first World Championships at the age of 16, she was quickly recognized as one of the teenage wonders of the Oksana Baiul generation.

Tanja had set her sights on stardom from the age of three, when she told her parents that she wanted to be world champion and tour with the famous European ice show "Holiday on Ice". She first made headlines at the 1994 Olympic Winter Games, where she collided with Oksana Baiul during a practice session there. Baiul went on to take gold and Tanja placed sixth at her first Olympics. Two

months later she was standing on the winners' podium as the world bronze medalist.

She continued her success in 1995 with her second German national title, but a stress fracture in her right foot forced her to withdraw from the World Championships. Then, after beginning to feel tired and listless early in the 1996 season, Tanja was diagnosed with a serious blood disorder and for a while feared for her life as well as her skating career. The illness kept her out of action for a whole year, during which it was uncertain whether she would ever skate again.

However, after a year of intensive treatment and recuperation, she finally returned to her skating in the spring of 1997, and in autumn she won two ISU Champion Series events, going on to finish second behind Tara Lipinski in the ISU Grand Prix Final.

Going from strength to strength Tanja won back her German national title in 1997, and after she had taken the bronze at the 1998 European Championships, a place on the winners' podium at the Olympic Games in Nagano one month later looked within her grasp. But disaster struck yet again when she was forced to withdraw with flu. She competed at the World Championships a month later, but her health was not fully restored and she managed only ninth place.

Lack of physical fitness and financial problems kept Tanja out of the 1999 season,

"I know exactly what I want, but I'm not taking anything for granted."

Career Record

Personal

BORN: July 26, 1977

HEIGHT: 5ft 4in (163cm)

WEIGHT: 110lb (50kg)

Honors

1994, 1995 and 1997 German National Champion

1994 World Bronze Medalist

1997 ISU Grand Prix Final Silver Medalist

1998 ISU Champion Series Silver Medalist

1998 European Bronze Medalist

but she intends to make a comeback yet again in 2000 and has set her hopes on being able to compete again for an Olympic medal in 2002.

28

ICE PRINCESSES

ICE PRINCESSES

Vanessa Gusmeroli

FRANCE

COMING TO TERMS WITH SUCCESS

Vanessa Gusmeroli astounded the world in 1997 by taking the bronze medal in only her second World Championships from a field of many seasoned competitors. With her new-found stardom came the pressures to continue the momentum, and Vanessa has battled with her mental focus ever since.

"My personal goal is to be the Olympic champion in 2002 in Salt Lake City."

VANESSA GUSMEROLI FIRST STEPPED ON TO the international scene in 1996, when she was placed sixth at the World Junior Championships, going on to finish eighth and 14th in her first Senior European and World Championships respectively. It was only one year later that she astounded everyone by taking the bronze medal at the World Championships in Lausanne. Her overnight success story made her an instant contender

for an Olympic medal the following year.

Suddenly thrust into the limelight, Vanessa found the media attention that went with winning a world medal to be something of a distraction and performed poorly at the 1998 European Championships, falling to 11th place. At the Olympics, she managed to raise herself for the occasion to finish in sixth place, but placed 16th at the World Championships in Minneapolis a month later.

The 1999 season looked promising for Gusmeroli when she took the silver medal in the French National Championships, and she went on to finish fifth at the European Championships among a strong field of Russian ladies. She began to look as if she was ready for elite competitions again and able to cope with the pressures that went with them. Her long program was skated to music composed by Maxime Rodriguez, with the choreography portraying a cat burglar.

Although she did not take a place on the winners' podium at the 1999 World Championships, Vanessa skated to a commendable final fifth place after placing third in the short program. Her contemporary style and her great jumping ability clearly make her a contender for an Olympic medal in 2002, provided she can find the consistency in her performances and a stronger mental edge at the main events.

Although only Midori Ito and Tonya

Harding have ever successfully landed the triple axel, Gusmeroli surely has the ability to join these two ladies and plans to incorporate this jump in her programs in the lead-up to the Salt Lake City Games.

Vanessa is also a national waterskiing competitor and, having been the European Games champion in 1991, is still competing in the French nationals. She says it helps her to alleviate stress. Whether it's frozen or melted, this girl can handle water!

Career Record

Personal

BORN: September 19, 1978

HEIGHT: 5ft 3in (160cm)

WEIGHT: 106lb (48kg)

Honors

1997 World Bronze Medalist

1997 and 1999 French National Silver Medalist

1998 Olympic Winter Games – 6th

Left: 1998 Winter Olympics.

1999 European Championships

In what appeared to be an overnight success, Tatyana Malanina went from six years of virtual obscurity to becoming one of the dominant female skating forces of 1999.

"Realizing that people want the best for you has affected my skating. Before when I performed, I skated only for myself. Now I do it for the public."

TATYANA MALANINA BEGAN HER INTERNATIONAL career very late in life for a Ladies' singles skater. She started competing internationally when she was 19 and has only recently begun to reach her potential at 26 – an age when many skaters are thinking of retirement.

She grew up in a skating environment as her father, a former skater and ice dancer, was a coach, while her mother was a former gymnast. Tatyana herself was hooked on figure skating from the first time she stepped on to the ice.

Originally from Russia, when the Soviet Union broke up she chose to go and skate for the former Soviet Republic of Uzbekistan, where she has been the national champion since 1993. In six World Championships from 1993, her best result was 13th in 1996 and many people believed that she was now too old to make the big break into the top group in world competition.

14th placing at Minneapolis a year earlier – and had become one of the *grandes dames* of the frozen stage. In looking at the support systems her fellow competitors had been enjoying over the years, with their facilities, top coaching and respected choreographers, it is amazing to see how Malanina has risen

Tatyana Malanina

■ UZBEKISTAN

THE CINDERELLA STORY OF THE DECADE

Left: 1998 Winter Olympics.

In the 1998–99 season, however, Tatyana burst on to the international scene with performances of remarkable consistency. She won her sixth national title and was unbeatable in the next four international events she entered, winning gold in two of the ISU Grand Prix events and going on to take the title at the ISU Grand Prix Final. In the inaugural Four Continents Championships she took gold again and looked unstoppable.

While many people were astounded at Tatyana's phenomenal improvement in just one year, she herself attributed her newfound success to having changed training bases after her national federation agreed to cover the costs for her to train at one of the top facilities in America. She has been training in Virginia since August 1998 and says her whole mental outlook has changed since she left Russia.

At the 1999 World Championships in Helsinki, Tatyana again performed to a high standard to finish fourth – 10 higher than her

to the challenge of competing with them.

Her consistent and superb jumping ability and her new mental focus, have been factors in her recent leap to the top. She has stated her desire to remain eligible and challenge again for that world title.

1999 European Championships.

Julia Soldatova

FOLLOWING IN THE FOOTSTEPS OF HER COUNTRYMEN

Julia Soldatova displayed no inhibitions in making the leap from the junior to the senior rankings. As the 1998 World Junior Champion, she went straight into the bronze medal position at her first World Championships the following year.

Above: 1999 European Championships.

Right: 1998 Winter Olympics.

JULIA SOLDATOVA BURST ON TO THE INTERnational scene like a whirlwind with a purpose. In her first World Championships in 1999, she leapt straight on to the podium, taking the bronze medal behind Maria Butyrskaya and Michelle Kwan – two women with vast experience at that level of the sport. Just prior to these Championships she had taken second place at the European Championships in Prague. Her performances at both these events, when she beat several experienced and high-ranking skaters, proved her status as a force to be recognized.

Soldatova's mother had been a skater, but not at a competitive level. She loved the sport and eagerly took her daughter to the local ice rink in Moscow when she was just four years old, hoping that her daughter would take to the ice and enjoy the sport as

Tchaikovskaya enhanced Julia's presentation skills by instilling emotion and expression in her performances.

she had. Take to the ice is just what she did, and by the age of 14 she was already representing Russia in junior international competitions. In 1997 she became the European Youth Olympic Winter Games champion.

It wasn't until the 1998 World Junior Championships that Julia first caught the attention of her audience and judges, winning that event and going on to take the Junior Grand Prix Final title that same year.

In March 1998 Julia began working with Elena Tchaikovskaya, who was guiding the successful career of Maria Butyrskaya. The change was a beneficial one, for Tchaikovskaya managed to develop a consistency in Julia's jumping technique and enhanced her presentation skills by instilling emotion and expression in her performances. These were two aspects that had been criticized in the past by her national federation.

At the 1999 Russian nationals, in one of the strongest Russian Ladies' events of all time, Soldatova secured the silver again, behind fellow teammate Maria Butyrskaya. It was indeed a coup for her coach to take the top two places at this event. The competition was especially fierce because the top six ladies were all competing for three places on the world team.

With her National Championship titles and two major international championship medals in her first year out, it is safe to say that Julia Soldatova has booked herself a place in the

battle for the next Olympic title in 2002. Training alongside the world champion, Maria Butyrskaya, in Moscow, she is in reputable company and her motivation should remain high. Julia will be looking to challenge for the world title in the not-too-distant future.

Career Record
Personal

BORN: May 17, 1981

HEIGHT: 5ft 3in (160cm)

WEIGHT: 101lb (46kg)

Honors

1998 World Junior Champion

1998 and 1999 Russian National Silver Medalist

1999 European Silver Medalist

1999 World Bronze Medalist

Lucinda Ruh's formidable spinning abilities excite and astound her audiences everywhere. Her inability to jump all the triples is the only factor keeping her away from the medals.

SWITZERLAND
Lucinda Ruh

CARRYING THE SWISS TRADEMARK TO HIGHER LEVELS

Above: 1998 Winter Olympics.

Right: 1998 World Championships.

LUCINDA RUH MAY NOT YET HAVE ESTABlished herself within the world's top 10, but it can safely be said that she is one of the best spinners the world of figure skating has ever seen. The Swiss have had a reputation as formidable spinners, ever since Denise Biellmann invented the spin named for her, and Ruh has taken this national trademark to new levels. If competitions were marked on spins alone, this young Swiss girl would be scoring perfect sixes.

Lucinda has lived in many different countries, as her father's career with a major chemical corporation has taken the family around the world. Born in Zurich, she lived in Paris before moving to Tokyo when she was just four years old, and today she speaks four languages fluently.

Beginning her skating career in Japan, she was fortunate to have Nobuo Sato,

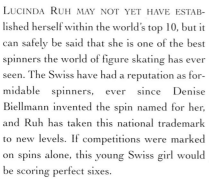

"I have not reached my full potential yet. I am a late bloomer."

father of world champion Yuka Sato, as her coach. It was Nobuo Sato who used spins as a means to assist Lucinda with the centering of her jumps, practicing the spins as a way of gaining confidence. Her weakness even today is an inability to hit the major triples in competition.

She had always been near the middle of the field in international events when, at 17, she moved to Toronto to work with Toller Cranston and Ellen Burka. Cranston choreographed two spectacular programs for Ruh that year, and when she skated in the Grand Prix Skate Canada event she won her first international medal – a bronze. This gave her a taste for success and she decided to move to San Francisco to be coached by Christy Ness, who had taken Kristi Yamaguchi to Olympic gold in 1992.

She had her best result yet at the World Championships of 1999 in Helsinki where, skating two excellently presented programs, she finished in 13th place. The audience's appreciation of her style and spins was evident in their response at the end of her performances. From then on, she has retained her ability to please the crowds. She was asked to skate in the "European Stars on Ice" tour, in which the producers had her skating in the middle of the show. However, the standing ovations she received each night soon persuaded the tour operators to change the running order, and she was selected to

skate at the end for the remainder of the tour – in the spot normally given to the headliners of the show.

Lucinda has said that she is still capable of completing all the triple jumps and has remained eligible to compete in 2000. She believes she will be able to crack the top group once she has established herself as a strong jumper as well as a spinner. When she finishes her skating career, she plans to go to medical school to become a physician specializing in sports medicine.

Career Record
Personal

BORN: July 13, 1979

HEIGHT: 5ft 7in (170cm)

WEIGHT: 121lb (55kg)

Honors

1993 Swiss Junior National Champion

1996 Swiss National Champion

1999 World Championships – 13th

ICE PRINCESSES

Ice Princes  3

There has been vast growth in the artistic development of men's singles skating in recent years that has contributed to the discipline's increase in public following. The men of today's World and Olympic Championships are breaking new ground with their varying individual artistic endeavors.

The Russians have provided us with the classical romantic styles of Ilia Kulik and the two Alexeis; Urmanov and Yagudin. Their style is in complete contrast to Canada's Elvis Stojko, who has developed a more contemporary style incorporating the martial arts. Then there are the theatrical character portrayals performed by the Frenchman, Phillipe Candeloro. With such varying degrees of musical interpretation, both judges and audiences alike are being treated to a collage of new looks within the men's event.

In the midst of all this artistic development, it cannot go unmentioned that the athletic jumping demands of elite men's singles have also risen to unprecedented levels. At the 1999 World Championships in Helsinki, 11 quadruple jumps were attempted, some successful and some not. The men have mastered the triple jumps, even in combination, so it was a natural course of events to see the quadruples become more abundant. The quad is now the goal of every male skater wishing to become a world champion.

It will not be too long before the next generation of Ice Princes begins to land all the jumps in quadruple rotation and we will be sitting in amazement at the first quintuple.

(Left to right) Evgeni Pushenko, Alexei Yagudin and Alexandr Abt.

Alexei Yagudin

RUSSIA

THE MAN WITH THE GOLDEN TOUCH

1999 was the year of Alexei Yagudin. His consistent performances at all the international major events proved him to be one of the greatest male skaters the Russian nation has ever produced.

Alexei Yagudin receives Gold at the European Championships 1999.

WINNING COMPETITIONS HAS BECOME synonymous with the name Alexei Yagudin. In the 1998–99 season he dominated the men's event by winning nine of the 11 events he entered.

Alexei first established himself as an international star in 1996 when he won the World Junior title in Brisbane, and such was the talent of this young Russian that only one year later, aged 17, he took the bronze medal on his debut at the World Championships in Lausanne.

Alexei was four and a half when his mother, Zoya, first took him to the local ice rink in St Petersburg, where he lived with his parents in a small apartment, sharing kitchen and bathroom facilities with two other families. It was fortunate that the Russian system footed the bill for his skating endeavors, for the family themselves had no means to meet such financial commitments.

A brilliant technician on the ice, Alexei was

quickly excelling at the jumps and technical components of the sport. In 1994, when his current coach left for a job in Sweden, Alexei took up with the legendary Alexei Mishin, who also coached the 1994 Olympic champion, Alexei Urmanov. Under Mishin's guidance, Yagudin developed into one of the leading men of the Russian skating empire, going on to become the first Russian man to take the World title in 1998 and, at 18, the second-youngest man in the world ever to do so.

To much surprise, shortly after the 1998 World Championships, Yagudin left Professor Mishin and changed to the world-famous Russian ice dance coach, Tatiana Tarasova, who was renowned for her ability to assist skaters in achieving their full potential. Aware that he needed to develop his style and presentation, Alexei felt that Tarasova was the person to assist with these endeavors. He yearned for a more individualized coaching approach, which he knew was not possible with Mishin.

Training with Tarasova brought Alexei to the US, where he began training at the American Hockey and Ice Skating Center in Freehold, New Jersey, whose facilities there were a far cry from those Alexei had known in his homeland.

He prospered in his new environment, and his partnership with Tarasova paid off when he retained his European and World titles in 1999. He plans to become the 2002 Olympic champion in Salt Lake City and,

with his immense talent and foresight for improving himself, Olympic gold seems to be the next natural step for this young Russian.

"I start to understand what I have to do, which work I have to do. Now it's like my job."

Career Record
Personal

BORN: March 18, 1980

HEIGHT: 5ft 8in (175cm)

WEIGHT: 139lb (63kg)

Honors

1996 World Junior Champion

1998 and 1999 European Champion

1998 and 1999 World Champion

1999 Grand Prix Final Champion

1999 World Professional Champion

Right: Alexei Yagudin at the World Championships in 1999.

"I don't want to wait . . . I already want to start winning."

The road to excellence in elite sport is usually long and filled with trials. From a poor Russian family background, Evgeni Plushenko is making a swift journey along this road.

Evgeni Plushenko

RUSSIA

IN PURSUIT OF EXCELLENCE

Above: 1998 European Championships.

Left: World Championship 1998.

EVGENI PLUSHENKO'S RISE TO THE TOP of the world has occurred at lightning speed. Just two years after becoming World Junior Champion in 1997, at the age of 14, he stood on the winners' podium at the World Championships in Helsinki, accepting the silver medal behind fellow Russian, Alexei Yagudin.

Evgeni took his first steps on to the ice at the age of four in his birthplace of Volgograd, formerly known as Stalingrad. His first coach was Mikhail Markaveyev, a former Russian weight lifter who was credited with establishing Evgeni's physical condi-

tioning and technique for jumping. Markaveyev coached Evgeni until 1993, when the breakdown of the former Soviet regime forced the rink in Volgograd to close.

At 11, he joined the famous Russian coach, Alexei Mishin, moving with his mother to St Petersburg, where they lived for five years in a one-room communal apartment. Family funds were so scarce in those days that Mishin himself assisted with the rent and living costs He could already see that it would not be long before this young Russian developed into one of the best skaters in the world.

By the time he was 13, Evgeni was already demonstrating all the triple jumps in his training sessions. He had also developed the skill to be able to execute the Biellmann spin, making him the first male skater to accomplish what had predominantly been known as an enhanced spin of the Ladies event. Today this spin is a regular feature of his competitive programs and delights his audiences whenever he performs it.

Evgeni's main competition at European and World Championships has come from his Russian teammates, with both the 1998 and 1999 European Championships seeing a clean sweep of the medals by the Russian men. It was Evgeni, at the tender age of 16, who won the Russian National Championships beating the reigning world champion, Alexei Yagudin, and the 1994 Olympic champion, Alexei Urmanov. Just months before he had also defeated three-time world champion, Elvis Stojko, in an event held in Stojko's native Canada.

So Plushenko was certainly a contender for the title at the 1999 World Championships in Helsinki. He was leading after the short program and planned to complete the quadruple toe-loop/triple toe-loop combination in his long program. Unfortunately for Evgeni, though, it was Yagudin who retained the title he had earned in 1998, leaving Plushenko to settle for the silver. Evgeni's youth, determination and talent will see him return to challenge for the title in 2000 and then move forward, with hopes of becoming the next Russian Olympic champion in Salt Lake City.

Career Record

Personal

BORN: November 3, 1982

HEIGHT: 5ft 10in (178cm)

WEIGHT: 130lb (59kg)

Honors

1997 World Junior Champion

1998 and 1999 European Champion

1999 Russian National Champion

1999 World Silver Medalist

Michael Weiss's greatest source of motivation and inspiration is his close-knit family of former elite sportspersons.

EVER SINCE WINNING THE WORLD JUNIOR title in 1994, Michael Weiss had looked a likely heir to the US Men's national title, although it was not until January 1999 in Salt Lake City that he finally lived up to the vast public expectation.

Behind this versatile and dynamic skater is one of the strongest and most experienced

winning six US National Championships.

The lifestyle of elite sport is something the Weiss family embrace wholeheartedly. With Michael the only family member still competing on an international level, the others are able to provide invaluable knowledge and support that enhances his career.

He began skating relatively late in life

Versatile and dynamic.

Michael Weiss

THE AMERICAN HERO

support teams in sport. His father, Greg, was a US Olympic gymnast who competed in the 1964 Olympic Games in Tokyo, and his mother, Margie, was also a national gymnast, now serving as the director of off-ice conditioning at the Fairfax Ice Arena where her son trains. Michael's two older sisters are also no strangers to the sporting arena. The first Weiss to take to the ice was Geremi Weiss Dalrymple, a US national medalist at the junior level, while the oldest sister, Genna, was a world junior diving champion,

when, after watching his sister skate, he decided he wanted to have a go. His coach for the last 14 years has been Audrey Weisiger, who is considered one of the top technical coaches in the world and was the driving force behind Michael's achievement of the quadruple jumps that he has demonstrated over the years. He is the first American man to land a quad in competition.

In September 1997, at the age of 21, Michael married his jazz instructor, Lisa Thornton, and a year later they celebrated the arrival of their daughter, Annie Mae. Together with Brian Wright, Lisa is involved in the choreography of Michael's competition programs and exhibition numbers.

Weiss placed a commendable seventh in his first Olympic Winter Games in 1998. After winning his national title a year later, he was still not considered a sure-fire contender for a world medal in Helsinki, where all eyes were cast on the Russians and the Canadian, Elvis Stojko. Yet Michael came through, surprising everyone with his consistent performances throughout the Championships and taking the world bronze medal behind Alexei Yagudin and Evgeni Plushenko, both of Russia.

Starting a family of his own seems to have helped Michael in his training and competing. There is now another side to his life that brings immense happiness and balance. He has stated his desire to continue through to Salt Lake City in 2002, where he will challenge for the Olympic title on US soil.

"I enjoy the dedication of my support system, composed of my family and training staff. My rise in the skating world and my satisfaction with my life and skating are due in a large part to this close-knit group."

Career Record

Personal

BORN: August 2, 1976

HEIGHT: 5ft 8in (173cm)

WEIGHT: 158lb (72kg)

Honors

1994 World Junior Champion
1998 Olympic Winter Games – 7th
1999 US National Champion
1999 World Bronze Medalist

Right: World Championship 1999.

Ilia Kulik

RUSSIA

THE OLYMPIC CHAMPION

The power to be great in one's finest hour is an essential trait of a true Olympic champion.

ILIA KULIK HAS BEEN DESCRIBED AS A natural skater, a "skater's skater" and an innovator in the sport. His gold-medal Olympic programs at the 1998 Winter Games in Nagano possessed the makings of something magical. Although only 21 when he won the Olympics, Ilia has been around on the international scene since 1993, when he took the bronze medal at the World Junior Championships at the age of 16.

Apart from his astounding achievement in Nagano, Ilia's performance record is blemished with inconsistency. After his bronze medal at the World Juniors, he dropped to 11th the next year, but went on in 1995 to take the title. That same year, on the senior stage, he won the European Championships, only to find himself in fourth place two years later. He won a silver medal at the World Championships in Canada in 1996 and then the following year dropped off the podium into fifth place. Even after winning his Olympic title in February 1998, he was beaten at several of the new Pro-Am events he competed in through the remainder of that year.

But ask yourself what is the ultimate prize for any elite sportsperson in the world. It's the glory of Olympic gold. And when the chips were down, Ilia Kulik had the focus and edge over the other competitors on that big day. It is a title he will hold through the next Olympiad, leading to Salt Lake City in 2002.

Kulik was strategically clever in planning his Olympic preparations. In 1997, in pursuit of a new look and a better grasp on handling competition pressures, he changed coaches to Tatiana Tarasova. The two formed an excellent partnership as Tarasova took the natural talent of this young Russian and refined it into that of a seasoned professional in the space of one year, as well as proving to be an excellent influence on the development of his inner strength and mental focus. Kulik was like a man with a mission throughout the 10 days at the Games in Nagano and, until he completed the task, his commitment to winning was undaunted.

Since winning his Olympic title, he has remained an eligible skater, keeping his options open should he decide to defend his title in 2002. He continues to expand his artistic abilities and performs with the "Stars on Ice" tour in the US. He still competes in the new Open Pro-Am events, which give him the opportunity to test new ideas. He has recently decided he likes the city lights of Los Angeles and has chosen to make his US base there. His family back in Moscow visit him regularly when his schedule doesn't allow him to make it back to Russia.

Gold medal celebrations at Nagano.

Career Record

Personal

BORN: May 23, 1977

HEIGHT : 6ft 1in (185cm)

WEIGHT: 156lb (71kg)

Honors

1995 World Junior Champion

1995 European Champion
1997 and 1998

Russian National Champion

1998 Grand Prix Champion

1998 Olympic Champion

Left: 1998 Winter Olympics.

"I think it's better to show dramatic skating. It's what everyone calls art on ice, it's something that opens the soul and everyone loves it."

Elvis Stojko

CANADA

JUMPING BEYOND THE BOUNDARIES

In the face of initial criticism of his styling and presentation, Elvis Stojko has remained true to himself and emerged a champion several times over.

OVER THE YEARS THE BOUNDARIES OF innovation and athleticism in figure skating have constantly moved forwards, and Elvis Stojko is one of the individuals who has been at the forefront of that evolution during the 1990s. His extraordinary jumping ability has kept the sport and its elite competitors striving towards higher achievement.

In 1991, at the World Championships in Munich, Elvis was the first man in history to succeed in landing a quadruple toe-loop in combination with a double toe-loop — a feat which has been executed in competition by still only a select few. Six years later, at the 1997 Grand Prix Final in Paris, Elvis moved the boundaries again when he landed the first ever quadruple toe-loop in combination with a triple toe-loop. Several other men had been practicing this difficult technical display of strength and power, yet Elvis was the first man to do so under the watchful eyes of a judging

panel and several thousand spectators.

Elvis's list of championship titles and competition achievements demonstrates his true talent. He has remained at the top for almost a decade and still keeps developing each season. Yet with all this success there is one title which has twice eluded him: the Olympic title. His first Olympics were in 1992, when he was in the shadow of fellow Canadian Kurt Browning and placed seventh. Both the 1994 and 1998 Games saw him on the winners' podium, but not as the champion. He was second both times. In 1994, the judges preferred the more classical style of Russian Alexei Urmanov over Stojko's more contemporary look. Then in 1998, when he was listed as the favorite, a groin injury kept him from skating his personal best and the title went to yet another young Russian, Ilia Kulik.

Criticized in the past for his artistic capacity, Elvis never tried to follow in the footsteps of any skaters before him. He has been an individual who took his greatest qualities and strengths and incorporated them into his artistry. Strength, courage, honesty and sensitivity are all words that describe the person and the artist in him.

Elvis did not have the easiest of years in 1999 for, although he won his national title for the fifth time, he was not in the medals at the World Championships in Helsinki. New faces and younger athletes seemed to dominate the Men's event, and athletes who in the past had looked up to Elvis as their idol were

Above: Silver at Nagano.
Right: World Championships 1999.

now managing to beat him. He has remained eligible and may well still hunger for the Olympic title. Whatever his endeavors, he will continue to be recognized as one of the most influential skaters of the past decade.

"I've always been an individual. I have always believed in doing the right thing for the right reason, and for myself."

Career Record

Personal

BORN: March 22, 1972

HEIGHT: 5ft 7in (170cm)

WEIGHT: 156lb (71kg)

Honors

1994, 1996–99
Canadian National Champion

1994 and 1998
Olympic Silver Medalist

1994, 1995 and 1997
World Champion

1997 Grand Prix Final Champion

49

Left behind in his wake as an eligible skater lies a legacy of character portrayals that figure skating will remember for a long time.

Candeloro the Barbarian.

CONAN THE BARBARIAN, LUCKY LUKE, The Godfather, Napoleon and d'Artagnan are all images that readily come to mind when one thinks of the 1994 and 1998 Olympic bronze medalist, Phillipe Candeloro. Although, as an amateur, he including swimming and trampolining but, soon after his ability on the ice shone through, his parents made him select one sport on which to focus his attentions. He chose to concentrate on skating — and only five years later was representing his country

Phillipe Candeloro

FRANCE

THE FLAMBOYANT FRENCHMAN ON ICE

never won a European, World or Olympic title, the impact this flamboyant Frenchman made on the world of skating has surpassed many of those who have attained the titles.

Strangely, Candeloro's portrayal of famous film characters on ice arose from his initial lack of enthusiasm for the artistic side of figure skating. As a teenager, he loved the speed and acrobatics of jumping in skating but was reluctant to delve into any artistic expression, worried that his peers at school would view this endeavor as "sissy stuff". Hence when he first started to please the crowds and judges alike with his character innovations, he found an avenue to express himself on the ice that was both comfortable and enjoyable.

Phillipe first came to the sport when his school took part in a skating program at the local ice rink in Colombes, where the resident coach, Andre Brunet, noticed the flair this young boy had for the ice. He approached the school and Phillipe's parents to sign him up for some private skating lessons, and has remained his coach ever since. At the time, Phillipe was involved in a host of sports,

at the 1985 World Junior Championships.

From that initial international assignment through to his bronze medal at the 1998 Olympic Winter Games, Phillipe's career has seen many highs and lows. He has suffered injury problems and faced disagreements with his national skating federation over the payment of prize money due to him. Yet in an international career that has spanned 14 years, he has attained four national titles, two European medals, two world medals and his two Olympic bronzes.

Candeloro turned professional almost immediately after stepping off the winners' podium in Nagano. His innate ability to connect with his audiences and demonstrate showmanship to the highest level make him a dominant force on the professional circuit. He plans to enjoy his professional status, free from the restriction of the amateur world, and has already produced his first full professional ice show in France. He married his choreographer, Olivia Darmon, in 1998, in a ceremony that took place on the ice at the Bercy Stadium in Paris.

Career Record

Personal

BORN: February 17, 1972

HEIGHT: 5ft 7in (170cm)

WEIGHT: 138lb (63kg)

Honors

1993–96 French National Champion

1993 and 1997 European Silver Medalist

1994 World Silver Medalist

1994 and 1998 Olympic Bronze Medalist

1995 World Bronze Medalist

Right: Playing d'Artagnan.

Candeloro's portrayal of famous film characters on ice arose from his initial lack of enthusiasm for the artistic side of figure skating.

"If you love a sport,
if you have a passion for it,
then I think you set goals for
yourself. You have long-term
and short-term goals and you
try to achieve whatever
you can."

Few men in the history of skating have managed to come back after several years of defeat to stand on the world podium again. Todd Eldredge is one of those men.

DEVOTION AND PERSEVERANCE ARE characteristics that have brought Todd Eldredge some of the highest accolades of international figure skating. As a child in Chatham, Massachusetts, he would rise early in the morning, stand by his parents' bed in his pyjamas with his tiny black skates in his hands and ask when they could go to the ice rink.

Todd's international career has had two phases. Phase one started when he won the world junior title in 1988, following two years later with the first of his US national titles at

skated with a 104-degree fever, and made only fourth place at the Nationals. With wounded confidence, he left the sport for a while, returning with a renewed vigor and a single-mindedness that has since become his trademark.

The start of phase two began in 1995, when he won back his national title and then surprised many by winning a silver medal behind Canada's Elvis Stojko at the World Championships in Birmingham. A year later, in Edmonton, Todd became the world champion in one of the greatest Men's competi-

Above: World Championships 1998 – Men's free Skating.

Left: World Championships 1998 – Men's free Skating.

UNITED STATES OF AMERICA

Todd Eldredge

THE DETERMINATION AND ENDURANCE TO RISE AGAIN

the age of 19. It was only a year after his breakthrough at the Nationals that he won a bronze medal at the 1991 World Championships in Munich, presenting himself as a strong contender for a medal at the next Olympic Winter Games to be held in Albertville.

However, injury, illness and self-doubt played havoc with the next three competitive seasons. A back injury kept him out of the US Nationals in 1992, although his world medal from the previous year was enough to earn him a place in the US Olympic team. Not fully recovered at the Games, though, he finished in a disappointing 10th place.

Things were no easier for Todd in 1993, when he managed only sixth place at the National Championships. The next year he missed a place on the Olympic team, having

tions of all time, followng with silver medals at the next two consecutive World Championships.

When he won that world gold medal in 1996, he skated over to the barrier and placed the medal over his mother's head in a wonderful gesture of appreciation for all the sacrifices his family had made for him as a skater and a son.

So far the Olympic Games have eluded him, his performances in Nagano in 1998 earning him only fourth place. However, he remains eligible, despite having chosen not to compete in the 1999 US Nationals or World Championships, and has been participating in tours and Pro-Am events. Should he return to challenge for an Olympic medal in 2002, then we may well see a phase three to this young man's incredible talents.

Career Record

Personal

BORN: August 28, 1971

HEIGHT: 5ft 8in (173cm)

Honors

1988 World Junior Champion

1990, 1991, 1997 and 1998 US National Champion

1996 World Champion

Alexei Urmanov

ARRIVING AHEAD OF SCHEDULE

Alexei Urmanov took the Olympic gold four years earlier than he had expected. A serious groin injury and the pressures of the sport have kept this young Russian from being able to recapture that initial glory.

IN 1977, FIGURE SKATING WAS ONE OF THE most popular sports in the former Soviet Union, with many opportunities for children to take up the sport and practice time virtually free. It was then that four-year-old Alexei Urmanov took his first steps on to the ice, instantly falling in love with figure skating. He quickly proved to be an outstanding talent, and it was not long before this talent was brought together with that of the legendary Russian master coach, Professor Alexei Mishin. The partnership proved to be a success and Urmanov has remained under Mishin's guidance throughout his career.

A love of the arts is a passion for Alexei as well as a part of his Russian culture. This passion is reflected in his style on the ice, where he is known for his classical lines and balletic presentation. Not only a stylist, Urmanov is also recognized as a proficient technician when it comes to jumping and spinning, and back in 1991 he was the first man to land a clean quadruple toe-loop in a European Championships.

In an international competitive career that has spanned almost a decade, Urmanov managed to achieve every elite sports person's ultimate reward — an Olympic gold medal. At the 1994 Olympic Winter Games in Lillehammer, Norway, a surprised Alexei stood on top of the winners' podium in the official medal ceremonies, having beaten a formidable group of men which included two past Olympic champions, Brian Boitano and Viktor Petrenko. Urmanov had not planned on winning the 1994 Games and prior to his win had been thinking more along the lines of the 1998 Games being his target goal. Not yet 21 years old, he had achieved the highest recognition in sport.

After his swift rise to the top, Alexei still had the desire to remain in the eligible rankings and pursue the dream of a second Olympic gold in Nagano. However, he did not always perform consistently and the pressures of being an Olympic champion sometimes got the better of him. The closest Alexei got to obtaining the world title was at the 1997 World Championships, where he was in the lead going into the long program before being forced to withdraw. He has been the Russian national champion five times consecutively; he has been European champion; he won the inaugural Grand Prix Final event in 1996; and of course he has the Olympic title of 1994. Yet that world title has so far eluded him.

He has always remained loyal to his country, staying close to his family and friends in St Petersburg when many other Russian skaters have abandoned the ice rinks of Russia for better facilities in North America. True to himself, he feels most comfortable back in his homeland.

Above: 1999 European Championships.

Left: 1999 European Championships.

Career Record

Personal

BORN: November 17, 1973

HEIGHT: 5ft 11in (180cm)

WEIGHT: 158lb (72kg)

Honors

1992–96 Russian National Champion

1994 Olympic Champion

1996 Grand Prix Final Champion

1997 European Champion

Steven Cousins

THE ULTIMATE SHOWMAN

The response to Steven Cousins's performances is often likened to that of pop stars. His charismatic nature and good looks make him a crowd favorite wherever he performs.

1998 Winter Olympics, Japan.

STEVEN COUSINS HAS HAD ONE OF THE longest reigns as British national champion. In nine consecutive years he has lost the title only once — in 1996 to the young Irish skater, Neil Wilson.

Although Steven has never won a major international championship medal, for a decade now he has remained one of the top audience attractions of his time. He possesses a charm and sincerity that, together with his striking good looks and provocative style, have catapulted him to the skating world's equivalent of pop-star status.

Steven began his skating career at his local ice rink in Deeside in Wales, when he and his older brother discovered it was the place where all the pretty girls would hang out. At first he did not enjoy the falling-down aspect of learning to skate, but before long he began to demonstrate a real talent and

"I know I can do it. It's just making sure that I can do it on the day. It just comes about from being happy and being happy with myself and playing my game, not anybody else's."

Left: 1998 Winter Olympics, Japan.

flair for the sport. His first coach, Donna Gately, guided him through to his first British national title in 1989, at the age of 17. Gately recognized that her protégé had the potential for international success and soon advised Steven to look abroad for better training facilities and a more elite environment than Wales had to offer.

Steven first went on to train with Alec McGowan, the coach who took Debi Thomas to her Olympic bronze medal and world title in the late eighties. After a few years he moved again to coaches Doug Leigh and Robert Tebby at the Mariposa School in Barrie, Ontario, where the arrangements were ideal for him. The coaching was the best he had experienced and he was put on daily training alongside the world champion, Elvis Stojko. He set up permanent residence in Canada and became romantically involved with the Canadian ice dancer, Shae-Lynn Bourne.

He has had some very near misses with regard to European and world medals, for example taking fourth place at the 1996 European Championships ahead of France's Phillipe Candeloro and Russia's Alexei Yagudin. He was also placed fifth after the short program at the Worlds that year, but a below-par long left him 15th overall. His best season was 1998, when for the first time he performed consistently well at all his major events, winning his eighth national title, being placed sixth both at the European Championships and at the Olympic Games, and taking seventh place at the World Championships.

Like many of his counterparts from the Nagano Games, Steven has kept the doors of opportunity open for himself and remained eligible, although he did not compete in the 1999 season of eligible events, skating instead in the US "Stars on Ice" tour.

Career Record

Personal

BORN: May 24, 1972

HEIGHT: 6ft (183cm)

Honors

1989–95 and 1997
British National Champion

1998 Olympic
Winter Games – 6th

Laurent Tobel

A COMEDIC APPROACH
TO THE ELIGIBLE PERFORMANCE

Conforming to the norm is not a feature of Laurent Tobel's contemporary style of skating. He has assisted in narrowing the gap between the eligible and the professional with a style that is truly original.

IT WAS AT THE 1997 WORLD CHAMPIONSHIPS in Lausanne that the skating world had the pleasure of being introduced to the unconventional skating of France's Laurent Tobel. His uniquely comical style of presentation was like a breath of fresh air as he performed his now infamous routine to the theme of The Pink Panther. Although his performance there resulted in only 13th place from the judges, he had instantly become one of the crowd favorites.

Tobel is currently the tallest man on the eligible Men's singles circuit at 6ft 3in. Despite his great height, he is able to execute cleanly all the "big gun" tricks of the sport that the very top men are producing. He even has a quadruple jump in his repertoire of skating skills. But it is not the jumps, spins and footwork that inspire Laurent to skate, for he finds the technical elements alone to be "rather flat". For him the true challenge of the sport is com-bining those elements with original choreography. His goal is not to convey any specific message through his choreography, but rather to skate in such a way as to provide the most pleasure possible to his fans and skating audiences. He feels that the eligible events should provide as much entertainment as can be found in the professional ranks.

After his initial appearance in 1997, Tobel questioned his own newly established style and, trying to conform more to what the masses were skating to, he changed his look in the 1998 season. A fall of three places at the World Championships then indicated that his original style was both what the audience wanted to see him skate to and what he was most comfortable with. So he returned in 1999 as the French national champion with his original Pink Panther program, came fifth at the European Championships, and followed with eighth in the World Championships two months later.

Since his ascent into the top 10 in the world, Laurent has been exciting American fans with his performances in the "Champions on Ice" tour. A crowd-pleaser par excellence, he prefers to skate exhibitions with an element of humor, so as not to bore the audience, and has been inspiring heartfelt laughter in his newly exposed exhibition program portraying a diaper-clad baby with a dummy. He has stated that he would like to remain eligible up to the 2002 Games in Salt Lake City, and beyond that would like to pursue a professional career of great longevity.

"Some judges do not understand my style."

Above: 1999 European Championships.
Right: 1999 European Championships.

Career Record

Personal

BORN: June 24, 1975

HEIGHT: 6ft 3in (188cm)

WEIGHT: 185lb (84kg)

Honors

1999 French National Champion

1999 European Championships – 5th

1999 World Championships – 8th

Takeshi Honda

A STAR RISING IN THE EAST

Takeshi Honda's initial foundations for skating were developed in his native Japan. In pursuit of international success he has sought North American facilities and coaching that have helped him develop into the best Japanese skater since Midori Ito.

TAKESHI HONDA'S RISE TO THE TOP SIX IN the world has taken place at lightning speed. He first came on to the senior international stage at the 1996 World Championships, where he was the youngest ever Japanese champion of any discipline.

Initially, Takeshi started short-track speed skating with his brother, but soon changed to figure skating at the age of nine. His instant display of talent gained him a place to train at the Tohoku High School in Sendai, which was some distance from the Honda family home in Koriyama. His mother eventually moved with him to Sendai so that he could benefit from regular training at the school. Training and living away from home proved very costly, and she was forced to take a job at a local grocery store to help supplement the family income, although once Takeshi made the Japanese national team, his federation assisted with the funding of his training.

After his debut at the World Championships in 1996, where he placed a commendable 13th,

Takeshi became the new hope for Japan. Not since Midori Ito, back in 1992, had the Japanese secured a major international medal. In 1997, as Takeshi moved up the world rankings to 10th, his federation felt he would benefit from training at one of the high-performance centers in America. So for 1998 Honda's talents were fostered by the International Ice Training Center of Connecticut in Simsbury and by Olympic coach Galina Zmievskaya, who was well known for her guidance of Olympic champions Viktor Petrenko and Oksana Baiul.

However, 1998 saw Takeshi fall out of the top 10 to 11th place at the World Championships in Minneapolis, and it was not long after this that he decided to change training bases again, this time heading north to Canada to join Canadian coach Doug Leigh. Leigh had produced world champions Brian Orser and Elvis Stojko in the past, and his Mariposa School of Skating was famous for its herd of elite male skaters from all over the world. The move proved beneficial for Honda, and only months later he became the Four Continents champion at the 1999 inaugural event in Halifax, Nova Scotia. This earned him the sole place on the Japanese team for the World Championships the following month.

Honda will undoubtedly be a major challenger for the next Olympic title in 2002, and his youth will also see him through to 2006, when he will be 25. His development since that first World Championships as a 14-year-old has demonstrated he has the makings of a future World and Olympic champion. His long-term goal is to be the Olympic champion in 2002.

Honda will be a major challenger for the next Olympic title in 2002, and his youth will see him through to 2006.

Above: 1999 European Championships.
Right: 1999 European Championships.

Career Record

Personal

BORN: March 23, 1981

HEIGHT: 5ft 6in (168cm)

WEIGHT: 128lb (58kg)

Honors

1996 and 1997
Japanese National Champion

1999 Four Continents Champion

1999 World Championships – 6th

61

Timothy Goebel

TEENAGE SENSATION

Multiple rotations in the air are a signature trademark of Timothy Goebel's athletic style of skating.

Out-jumping the older kids.

HE MADE SKATING HISTORY AT THE AGE OF 17, when he became the first skater ever to land a quadruple salchow in official competition at the 1998 ISU Junior Series Final in Lausanne, Switzerland. This feat also made history back in the US, and Goebel also became the first American to land a quadruple jump in competition. Landing the quad and taking the gold medal in Lausanne catapulted Goebel into the new group of elite skaters who are taking the sport of figure skating to unprecedented levels of athletic achievement.

It was public sessions at the age of four when Timothy first began skating. During his childhood he was also involved in gymnastics and karate, but his talent and love for figure skating soon took precedence. By 14, Timothy was already achieving national acclaim when he won the 1994 US Novice title. That same year he was selected by his governing body to skate in the US Olympic Festival where he won a silver medal.

Goebel wasted no time moving up the national ladder in the Junior rankings. In 1995 he was fifth and the following year he became the US Junior Champion. Goebel started to amass international recognition. In his 1996/7 season, he won two silver medals at ISU Junior Series events and took the silver at the World Junior Championships in St Johns, Canada. That year he moved up into the Senior National rankings at the US Championships and debuted in sixth place.

Goebel started the 1997/98 season with explosive dominance at the Junior internationals. He won gold at his two ISU Junior Series assignments in France and the Ukraine and looked destined for the World Junior title. Injury to muscles surrounding his left hip dashed Goebel's attempt to capture the Junior title when he had to withdraw after the initial rounds of the competition. The injury also kept him out of the 1998 US Nationals, preventing any attempt at improving on his sixth-place finish of the year before.

Only two months after the 1998 US Nationals, Timothy Goebel returned to the competitive arena and made his historic jump in Lausanne, winning the coveted ISU Junior Series Final. The next season, he took the bronze medal at the 1999 US Championships earning Timothy his first US World Team place. He went on to place 12th at his first World Championships in Helsinki.

We are certain to see much more of this tremendous teenage jumping sensation. Goebel plans to be at the 2002 Olympic Winter Games in Salt Lake City.

"I think I've started to become more of a threat to the older kids – we're pretty much equal right now, though I think I have an edge in the technical aspect of jumping."

Career Record
Personal

BORN: September 10, 1980

HEIGHT: 5ft 7in (170cm)

WEIGHT: 130lb (59kg)

Honors

1997 World Junior Silver Medalist
1998 ISU Junior Series Champion
1999 US Championships
Bronze Medalist

Great Double Acts

4

I t is the Russian partnerships that have dominated world pairs skating and ice dancing for the past three decades. Their highly romantic style, reminiscent of the famous Russian ballet has been a contributing factor to their success. They are able to form a unity in their teams that is unrivalled by other nations.

Like the men's singles event, world class pairs skating has taken quantum leaps in the development of athletic acrobatics. The pairs of today are performing feats of death defying nature, where they are taking throws and lifts to astounding new levels. In 1998, the world thought France's Sarah Abitbol and Stephane Bernadis would complete the first triple axel throw in competition but they were unsuccessful.

Although ice dance does not include all the acrobatic displays of the pairs, it has experienced its own major changes in the past few years. In an attempt to make the judging of the sport more objective, the ISU changed its regulations to include compulsory elements for demonstration in the original and free dance sections of the competition. This would provide the opportunity for the judges to mark these elements in a similar way to how the short programmes are judged in the singles and pairs. Failure to complete an element successfully would result in a deduction from the final score. This would help defer any speculation that the sport was being judged on a political level as was the feeling following the 1998 Olympic Games in Nagano.

The great double acts of today's competitive figure skating are innovators of their time. They are constantly pushing the boundaries of the sport in a quest to challenge what has gone before them.

Anjelika Krylova and Oleg Ovsyannikov.

Elena Berezhnaya
& Anton Sikharulidze

RUSSIA

GRACE AND POWER

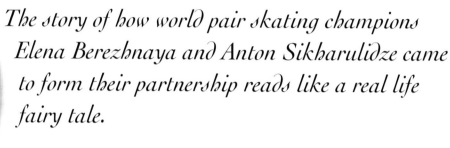

The story of how world pair skating champions Elena Berezhnaya and Anton Sikharulidze came to form their partnership reads like a real life fairy tale.

1999 World Championships, Helsinki..

IN JANUARY 1996, ELENA BEREZHNAYA WAS in a horrific training accident on the ice. While performing a side by side camel spin with her former partner, Oleg Shilakhov, Shilakhov's skate blade pierced through Elena's skull. She was rushed to the hospital where she underwent intensive surgery to remove bone debris from her brain. The accident resulted in damaged motor skills for Elena and she had to undergo extensive therapy in order to regain her ability to speak.

Prior to the accident, Elena with Shilakhov and Anton with his partner, Maria Petrova, had been training under legendary Russian pairs coach, Tamara Moskvina. Anton was falling in love with Elena and directly following her accident in Latvia he brought her back to St Petersburg to recover.

Four months later, Elena took her first tentative steps back on to the ice and began skating with Anton. Soon Elena regained her confidence and her new partnership looked destined for great things. Within a year, they won the bronze medal at the 1997 European

Championships. The partnership quickly flourished both on and off the ice. Their intimate style of grace and power was soon compared to the legendary pairs team of Ekaterina Gordeeva and Sergei Grinkov.

1998 marked Berezhnaya and Sikharulidze's ascent to the top of the podium. They were ranked as the number two couple of Russia but went on to win three major international championships that year and a silver medal at the 1998 Olympic Games in Nagano. It was hard to believe that a couple, together for only two years, was displaying a unity on the ice that normally took years for most couples to acquire.

In 1999, Elena and Anton won their first Russian national title. Elena contracted flu, forcing them to withdraw from the European Championships, and unable to defend their title. Consequently, in their absence the title was taken by Anton's ex-partner Maria Petrova and her new partner Alexei Tikhonov. Two months later, however, Elena and Anton did successfully defend their world title in a challenging battle with the new Chinese pair, Xue Shen and Hongbo Zhao, who had beaten them at that year's Champion Series Final.

Berezhnaya and Sikharulidze will be working towards gold at the 2002 Olympic Games in Salt Lake City. They want to continue to expand and grow as a pair both ath-

letically and artistically. But their ultimate goal is to leave a lasting mark on the world of figure skating that will be remembered for years to come.

Career Record
Personal

Elena
BORN: October 11, 1977
HEIGHT: 5ft 0in (154cm)
WEIGHT: 93lb (42kg)

Anton
BORN: October 25, 1977
HEIGHT: 6ft 0in (182 cm)
WEIGHT: 168lb (76kg)

Honors

1999 Russian
National Champions

1998 European Champions

1998 and 1999
World Champions

1998 Olympic Silver Medalists

1999 World Championships.

Big throws and jumps are the pair's trademark.

Xue Shen & Hongbo Zhao

CHINESE PIONEERS

They have been pairs partners since 1992 and have competed in five World Championships for China, yet it wasn't until late 1997 that Xue Shen and Hongbo Zhao came to world prominence by winning one of the ISU Grand Prix events: NHK Trophy in Japan.

World silver medalists in 1999.

THEIR BEST RESULT PRIOR TO THAT WIN WAS an 11th place finish at the 1997 World Championships in Lausanne. Since that initial breakthrough, this pair has gone from strength to strength. Both Shen and Zhao started skating as singles skaters. Zhao went into pairs, and when his first partnership did not appear to be going anywhere, the Chinese skating federation brought in Shen as a stand-in partner. They worked with Chinese national coach Bin Lao and were rewarded with a place on the national team the very next year.

China's only international success in figure skating had been with Ladies' singles skater Chen Lu who was the first Chinese skater ever to win an Olympic medal for her country. In the pairs skating discipline, China had never featured as a leading nation. Shen and Zhao's first World Championships in 1994 saw them in 21st place out of almost as many pairs.

Bin Lao had a plan for his pair and worked diligently to secure big throws and jumps that would later become the pair's trademark. Taking advantage of the couple's Chinese heritage, he developed a style that drew on Chinese ethnic dancing. This proved a great success in the 1999 season when their program to the music from Disney's *Mulan* won them China's first pairs international championships medal at the inaugural Four Continents Championships in Halifax.

Following their triumph in Halifax, Shen and Zhao went on to the 1999 Grand Prix Final in St Petersburg, beating the reigning world champions, Elena Berezhnaya and Anton Sikharulidze of Russia. This set the stage for an exciting pairs event at the World Championships a few weeks later. Although they skated better than they had at the Grand Prix Final, Shen and Zhao had to settle for the silver behind their Russian counterparts at the World Championship in Helsinki. Many of the spectators felt the Chinese couple had proven they were worthy of the title and rewarded Shen and Zhao with a standing ovation upon completion of their free program.

The 2002 Olympic Winter Games are high on the list of priorities for Shen and Zhao. They have become a dominant force in their chosen sport and are certain to push their competitors to higher levels over the years leading up to the Games.

Career Record

Personal

Xue
BORN: November 13 1978
HEIGHT: 5ft 3in (160cm)
WEIGHT: 99lb (45kg)

Hongbo
BORN: September 22, 1973
HEIGHT: 5ft 9in (176cm)
WEIGHT: 143lb (65kg)

Honors

1993–1994 and 1996–1999 Chinese National Champions

1999 Four Continents Champions

1999 Grand Prix Final Champions

1999 World Silver Medalists

Oksana Kazakova &
Artur Dmitriev

D E T E R M I N E D   C O U P L E

When Artur Dmitriev paired up with the relatively unknown Oksana Kazakova in 1995, the man had little left to prove in international figure skating.

Career Record

Personal

Oksana

BORN: April 8, 1975

HEIGHT: 5ft 2in (157cm)

WEIGHT: 95lb (43kg)

Artur

BORN: January 21, 1968

HEIGHT: 6ft 0in (183cm)

WEIGHT: 185lb (84kg)

Honors

1996 European Champions

1997 World Bronze Medalists

1998 Olympic Champions

1998 Russian Bronze Medalists

WITH HIS FORMER PARTNER, NATALIA Mishkutenok, Dmitriev had achieved European, World and Olympic titles in the early 1990s. But his passion for competing and the challenges sport holds motivated Dmitriev to embark on the road to Olympic gold once again.

At the end of the 1994 season, Dmitriev and Mishkutenok went their separate ways. Natalia wanted to pursue a professional career and Artur wanted to remain eligible. Early in 1995 Artur tried out with 19-year-old Oksana Kazakova, at first on their own, and then Artur sought the advice of his long-time coach, Tamara Moskvina. Moskvina could see the raw potential in the partnership and began working with the new team.

With Dmitriev's great strength and vast experience coupled with Kazakova's fearless determination, the team produced rapid results in the initial stages. After only one year together they won the 1996 European Championships.

At first 1997 seemed as if it was going to be a lost year for Oksana and Artur. A fourth-place finish in the Russian Nationals kept the pair from making the Russian team for the 1997 European Championships. It was only after they had won the silver at the Champion Series Final a few weeks later

European Championships, Milan 1998.

that the Russian federation agreed to put them on the world team for the March Championships in Lausanne. The decision proved profitable for the Russians when Kazakova and Dmitriev took the world bronze medal.

In the following year at the 1998 Games shortly after Artur's 30th birthday, this still relatively new partnership came to full fruition. They skated to near perfection at the Games and walked away with the title. It was Artur's third Olympic medal and his second title. It was Oksana's first Olympic Games ever and they had taken the gold.

Kazakova and Dmitriev remained eligible throughout the 1999 season and yet did not compete in the Russian, European or World Championships that year. Instead they chose to compete in only the new Pro-Am events and enjoy their Olympic Champion status. Perhaps they were testing the waters of the professional world to see if they were ready. Apparently so, as in June 1999 they announced their intention to turn professional. They will undoubtedly enjoy great success in the pro ranks with their crowd-pleasing style and innovative moves.

GREAT DOUBLE ACTS – PAIRS & ICE DANCE

Career Record

Personal

Jenni

BORN: November 19, 1970

HEIGHT: 5ft 0in (152cm)

WEIGHT: 96lb (44kg)

Todd

BORN: October 30, 1963

HEIGHT: 5ft 11in (180cm)

WEIGHT: 165lb (75kg)

Honors

1994–1996
US National Champions

1995–1996 World Bronze Medalists

1998 World Silver Medalists

Jenni Meno and Todd Sand's skating career and personal lives together evolved over three Olympic cycles. At the 1992 Olympic Games in Albertville, when both Jenni and Todd were skating with different partners, they fell in love.

THEN IN NORWAY, AT THE 1994 GAMES competing as the new US Champions, Todd proposed.

In their final Games of 1998 in Nagano, the duo skated as husband and wife. Only an Olympic medal eluded them each time, but the memories they share will be told to their children in years to come.

bronze medal in both the 1995 and 1996 World Championships.

The climate changed for Jenni and Todd in 1997. By the time the US Nationals came around, the added pressure of external expectations together with an injury to Todd's wrist resulted in the pair los-

Above: 1998 World Championships.

Left: NHK Trophy Osaka, Japan 1996.

UNITED STATES OF AMERICA

Jenni Meno & Todd Sand

FAVORITES OF THE FANS

Both Jenni and Todd began as singles skaters. Jenni's career took her all the way to competing for the prestigious US Ladies' title in 1989 and 1990. Todd, having dual citizenship with Denmark, was the Danish Champion from 1981 to 1983. Their career as pairs skaters developed with separate partners, Jenni with Scott Wendland and Todd teamed up with Natasha Kuchiki.

Jenni and Todd formed their partnership shortly after the 1992 World Championships, dominating the US pair scene from 1994 through 1996, taking the national title each year. They also took the

ing their US title to Kyoko Ina and Jason Dungjen. Problems followed Meno and Sand to the World Championships in Lausanne where they could only manage fifth place.

A dark cloud seemed to linger into the 1998 Olympic year. Jenni and Todd were forced to withdraw from the 1998 US Nationals due to injury. Nagano proved to be a nightmare for the now husband-and-wife team with the worst performance of their eligible career in the final of the pairs event resulting in their lowest international result ever – eighth place.

Then only a few weeks later, Meno and Sand found themselves in the number one position after the pairs short program at the 1998 World Championships in Minneapolis, finishing with the silver medal

On this high note, they decided to retire from the eligible scene. Todd was 34 and Jenni was 27. Some of the new pairs coming through were still in their teens. As professionals Jenni and Todd are real favorites of the skating fans. They have a unique closeness with one another that is expressed in their sense of unity – a feature of true pair champions.

Mandy Wotzel and Ingo Steur had each experienced international acclaim in pairs skating before they teamed up in 1992.

GERMANY

Mandy Wotzel & Ingo Steur

ICE AMBASSADORS

Above: 1994 Winter Olympics.

Right: 1997 World Championships.

AT JUST 15, MANDY HAD WON A SILVER medal at the 1989 European Championships with former partner, Axel Rauschenbach. Ingo was World Junior Champion in 1984 with his first partner, Manuela Langraf, and was ranked seventh in the world in 1990 with his second partner, Ines Mueller.

Following the break-up of their previous partnerships, the teaming of Wotzel and Steur proved to be an immediate success. After only a year of training together they won the German National title and went on to take silver medals at the European and World Championships that same year.

The years that followed their break-through on the world stage were riddled with various injuries suffered by both Mandy and Ingo. The pair had demonstrated that they were definite contenders for a world title and yet at several major events they were forced to withdraw due to injury.

In 1996, they won their second silver medal at the World Championships in Edmonton despite evident personal conflict surrounding the partnership. They sought the support of a top German sports psychologist to assist with their problems and competition focus and they changed choreographers for the 1997 season. The added support paid off and Mandy and Ingo enjoyed their best season, winning their fourth national title and both the Champion Series Final and World Championships of that season. They were now favorites for the Olympic gold the following season.

At the end of 1997, leading up to the Games in Nagano, disaster struck. Ingo was hit by a car while on foot and suffered a shoulder injury that forced the pair out of the European Championships the following

January. They arrived at the Games in February, still uncertain as to whether Ingo's shoulder would hold out in competition. Despite this, they achieved the goal they had set out for at these Games, taking a medal — the bronze, behind two Russian pairs, Oksana Kazakova and Artur Dmitriev and Elena Berezhnaya and Anton Sikharulidze.

Having won medals in all the major international championships for figure skating, Mandy and Ingo retired from eligible skating. They went on in 1999 to compete in the professional events and star in various tours in Europe and North America. They have a great desire do the same for German skating as it has done for them and the pair are strong European spokespersons for the sport. It is their wish to see figure skating back in their homeland enjoy the profile it does in America.

GREAT   DOUBLE   ACTS   –   PAIRS   &   ICE   DANCE

It has been more than 60 years since France has won a world medal in the pairs event. The last time was in 1932 when famed husband-and-wife team Andrée and Pierre Brunet took the title. Now for the first time in as many years, the French are excited about the prospects of their current team, Sarah Abitbol and Stephane Bernadis.

An electrifying combination.

FRANCE

Sarah Abitbol & Stephane Bernadis

FRENCH SPARKLERS

SARAH AND STEPHANE HAVE BEEN SKATING together since 1992 and have been the French National Pairs Champions since 1994. Both started skating as singles skaters; Sarah represented France at the 1993 World Junior Championships. It was during his late teens that Stephane started to look for a suitable partner with whom to venture into

"We feel good in the amateur world, and we have lots of things to prove — we hope to have results."
STEPHANE

the pairs arena. After several partners, including European Ladies Champion, Surya Bonaly, Stephane found Abitbol, the perfect match.

Sarah possessed the ideal physical characteristics of an elite female pairs skater. At just under five feet tall and packed with lean muscle, she could be lifted and thrown through the air in a spectacularly dynamic fashion. One of the main features of this French team's style is their great power and breathtaking throws.

The road to international recognition was slow at first and Sarah and Stephane floated around the middle of the field at World Championships during 1993 to 1997. Then in 1998, they started to show their true potential when they won the bronze medal at the European Championships and finished sixth and eighth at that year's Olympic Winter Games and World Championships respectively.

After the 1998 season, Sarah and Stephane changed coaches and started to work with the Russian coach, of legendary pair team, Ekaterina Gordeeva and Sergei Grinkov. Abitbol and Bernadis quickly took to the change and found themselves recapturing the bronze medal at the 1999 European Championships in Prague and moving up three more places to fifth at the World Championships in Helsinki.

They are one of the most electrifying pairs on the world circuit at this time, and have aims to become the first pair to successfully complete a triple axel throw, an achievement they have landed in practice but have yet to officially land in a competition. The law of averages tells us that Sarah and Stephane may soon accomplish that feat. In doing so, they will be pushing the technical and athletic demands of the sport to a higher level and leaving their imprint on the sport of figure skating forever.

Career Record

Personal

Sarah
BORN: June 8, 1975
HEIGHT: 4ft 11in (150cm)
WEIGHT: 95lb (43kg)

Stephane
BORN: February 23, 1974
HEIGHT: 5ft 10in (178cm)
WEIGHT: 172lb (78kg)

Honors

1994–1999
French National Champions

1996, 1998–1999
European Bronze Medalists

1998 Olympic Games – 6th

Anjelika Krylova
& Oleg Ovsyannikov

TRUE TO THEIR INSTINCTS

1998 World Championships.

In today's world of competitive ice dance, patience is a virtue. After spending four years in the shadows of twice Olympic champions, Pasha Grishuk and Evgeny Platov, Anjelika Krylova and Oleg Ovsyannikov finally stepped into the number one position at the 1998 World Championships in Minneapolis.

BOTH KRYLOVA AND OVSYANNIKOV WERE NO strangers to international ice dance when they formed in 1994. Krylova had previously skated with Vladimir Federov, winning a bronze medal at the 1993 World Championships. Ovsyannikov also took a bronze medal at the 1988 World Junior Championships with former partner Maria Orlova.

Krylova and Ovsyannikov's partnership received instant international acclaim when they came fifth in their first World Championships in 1995. The very next year they moved into the silver medal position behind fellow teammates Grishuk and Platov. They remained in that position for the next two years until the 1998 Games in Japan. Grishuk and Platov retired after the 98 Games and one month later Anjelika and Oleg were crowned the new world champions of ice dance.

It was not a foregone conclusion for Anjelika and Oleg when they repeated their success in 1999, adding the European and Champion Series Final titles to their names.

The 1999 season saw tough challenges from both of the world's number two couples, Marina Anissina and Gwendal Peizerat of France and Canada's Shae-Lynn Bourne and Victor Kratz. In their quest to push the boundaries of art in their sport, Krylova and Ovsyannikov's 1999 free dance was interpreted entirely to drum rhythms. There were mixed views from the judging panels on this innovative approach. Anissina and Peizerat had created a classical style free dance to music from *The Man with the Iron Mask*. It was felt that the judges might favor the French team over the Russians at the World Championships at the end of the year. Krylova and Ovsyannikov stayed true to their instincts and continued to develop their program through the season. By the World Championships in Helsinki, the speed and drama of the program saw them through to their second consecutive world title.

Anjelika and Oleg have not confirmed whether they will remain eligible until the next Olympic Games in 2002. They have said they will continue to compete until they feel they have nothing left to offer the amateur world, but are uncertain how long that will be. Today they live in the US where they train with famous Russian coach, Natalia Linichuk at the University of Delaware Arena. Both Anjelika and Oleg have become accustomed to the excellent training facilities America has to offer and look forward to retaining their title in 2000.

"It's not like it just came by itself ... We worked a lot to get this title."

OLEG

Career Record

Personal

Anjelika
BORN: July 4, 1973

HEIGHT: 5ft 8in(170cm)

WEIGHT: 123lb (56kg)

Oleg
BORN: January 23, 1970

HEIGHT: 6ft 0in (184cm)

WEIGHT: 165lb (75kg)

Honors

1995, 1998–1999
Russian National Champions

1998–1999 World Champions

1998 Olympic Silver Medalists

1999 European Champions

1999 Grand Prix
Final Champions

1999 World Championships.

1998 World Championships.

Career Record
Personal

Marina
BORN: August 30, 1975

HEIGHT: 5ft 4in (162cm)

WEIGHT: 103lb (47kg)

Gwendal
BORN: April 21, 1972

HEIGHT: 5ft 8in (173cm)

WEIGHT: 141lb (64kg)

Honors

1996–1999
French National Champions

1998–1999 World Silver Medalists

1998 Olympic Bronze Medalists

1999 European Silver Medalists

1999 Grand Prix
Final Silver Medalists

Marina Anissina and Gwendal Peizerat both started skating at the age of four. Skating was in their genes as Marina and Gwendal each descended from families with elite skating backgrounds.

1999 World Championships.

MARINA'S MOTHER, IRINA CHERNIYEVA, represented the Soviet Union at the 1972 Olympic Winter Games as a pairs skater. Gwendal's parents had both been ice dancers and his father is the General Secretary of the

World Junior Championships, with separate partners and representing different nations, that Marina and Gwendal first met. Marina won these championships with her then partner, Ilia Averbukh and Gwendal, skating with Marina Morel, finished in fourth place.

Two years later, Averbukh split from Marina and she suddenly found herself with all the passion and determination to skate but without a partner. In early 1993, Marina

style that reflects their separate heritages. In recent years they have advanced in artistic respects coming up with innovative moves, and creating thematic programs that have been the favorites with audiences. They have remained eligible and are looking to transform the color of their 1998 Olympic medal to a brighter shade in 2002.

FRANCE

Marina Anissina & Gwendal Peizerat

ASCENDING THE HEIGHTS

Fédération Française des Sports de Glacé – France's national governing body for the sport.

Marina's career began as a singles skater, but her mother, a coach at the time, persuaded her to take up ice dance at the age of 10. Irina felt the other disciplines were far more inclined to the risk of injuries and the artistic and theatrical elements of ice dance better suited her flamboyant young daughter. Gwendal knew only ice dance from his initial foundations in the sport. The local rink in Lyon was predominantly known for its dancing so it was natural for him to gravitate towards that discipline. He had his first partner at the tender age of eight.

It wasn't until each competed at the 1990

flew to Lyon to conduct a try-out with Gwendal that instantly showed potential.

The partnership ascended the world rankings in quantum leaps. They were 10th at their first World Championships in 1994 in Chiba, Japan. They continued their rise through 1995–1997. It was in the Olympic year of 1998, Anissina and Peizerat first stepped on to the international winner's podium, taking bronze at the Champion Series Final, the European Championships and the Olympic Winter Games. Several weeks later they took the silver medal at the World Championships in Minneapolis, a result they repeated the following year, adding the silver European medal as well.

Anissina and Peizerat possess a unique

"We try to do our best with many emotions, and we don't listen to what they say when judging. We just concentrate on our skating."
MARINA

GREAT DOUBLE ACTS – PAIRS & ICE DANCE

Shae-Lynn Bourne & Victor Kratz

IN SEARCH OF A CANADIAN DREAM

It had been eight years since Canada had won a world medal when Shae-Lynn Bourne and Victor Kratz took bronze at the 1996 World Championships in Edmonton.

Above: Inventors of hydroblading.

Left: Nova Scotia Free Dance 1997.

IT WAS THEIR FOURTH WORLD Championships together, and they had moved up the ranking with lightning speed from their 14th-place finish back in 1993. They have dominated the Canadian dance scene for seven years with no other couples in that time threatening their national title.

Shae-Lynn was a 16-year-old pairs skater when Victor was trekking through eastern Canada looking for a partner. He was introduced to Shae-Lynn, they had a trial week and they went on from strength to strength. Victor feels that Shae-Lynn's pairs-skating experience has helped bring new ideas to their partnership. Together with their former choreographer, Uschi Kezler, Bourne and Kratz are the inventors of a style of skating known as hydroblading. This involves leaning so far over on the edges that the skater's body is just inches above the ice. This innovative style is the trademark of most of the couple's performances.

In 1997, Shae-Lynn and Victor won their first major international event at the Champion Series Final. From there they went on to win their second world bronze medal that year in Lausanne, behind Russian couples, Oksana Grishuk and Evgeny Platov and

Anjelika Krylova and Oleg Ovsyannikov. Just behind Bourne and Kratz were the French National Champions Marina Anissina and Gwendal Peizerat. The approaching Olympic Games of 1998 looked as if it was going to be a fierce battle for the medals.

In what proved to be a highly controversial ice dance event at the Nagano Olympics, Bourne and Kratz were pushed off the podium by Anissina and Peizerat who took the bronze medal. There was vast speculation that the ice dance event at these Games had been judged in a political atmosphere, which saw supposed deals being struck with some of the nations' judges. Ice dancing received huge criticism following Nagano and the ISU made quick changes to the judging format and competition content for the future.

Shae-Lynn and Victor did not win their Olympic medal in 1998, but they went on to win the bronze medal yet again at the World Championships and then repeated this result in 1999. No Canadian ice dance couple has ever won an Olympic gold medal and it has always been Bourne and Kratz's dream to be the first. If they can continue to grow and develop as they have in the past decade, 2002 may well prove the realization of that dream.

Career Record

Personal

Shae-Lynn
BORN: January 24, 1976

HEIGHT: 5ft 4in (163cm)

WEIGHT: 117lb (53kg)

Victor
BORN: April 7, 1971

HEIGHT: 5ft 10in (178cm)

WEIGHT: 143lb (65kg)

Honors

1993–1999
Canadian National Champions

1996–1999 World Bronze Medalists

1999 Four Continents Champions

So strong is the Russian hold on the world of ice dance that making it on to the Russian national team almost guarantees a position among the top couples in the world.

IRINA LOBATCHEVA AND ILIA AVERBUKH have maintained a place on the Russian team for six years now. Quite a feat if you consider that they have only been skating together for seven years.

Ilia was the 1990 and 1992 World Junior Ice Dance Champion with former partner Marina Anissina. Anissina, now ranked second in the world with partner Gwendal Peizerat, represents France. During his partnership with Anissina, Ilia fell in love with Irina Lobatcheva, from a rival Russian dance couple. To Marina's disappointment Ilia left to skate with Irina. The change in partners was at first questioned as Averbukh and Anissina already enjoyed recognition on the international stage and looked to have huge potential for the future. But love conquered all and Ilia commenced training with Irina in 1993 and they were soon married.

By 1994, Lobatcheva and Averbukh were the number two Russian couple behind Olympic champions Oksana Grishuk and Evgeny Platov and came 13th in their first World Championships together. In 1995, the emergence of the newly formed couple Anjelika Krylova and Oleg Ovsyannikov saw Ilia and Irina drop to third nationally

and 15th in the world. Then in 1997, in the absence of both Grishuk and Platov and Krylova and Ovsyannikov, Irina and Ilia took the prestigious Russian National title. Their reign as champions did not last when Krylova and Ovsyannikov returned in

1998 European Championships.

1998 to take their title away and retain it the following season.

It was 1999, when Irina and Ilia really made an impact. At the European Championships in Prague, they won the bronze medal just behind Ilia's former partner Marina Anissina and her partner Gwendal Peizerat. Then at the World Championships two months later Irina and Ilia held on to their fourth-place finish in 1998, and appeared to put the pressure on the couples in front of them.

Irina and Ilia have set their sights on the gold medal in Salt Lake City in 2002. They have dreams of becoming the fourth married ice-dance couple to win an Olympic title. They believe that their partnership off the ice helps to strengthen their unity on the ice. They have lived and trained in the US since 1995 at the renowned University of

Delaware arena alongside world champions Krylova and Ovsyannikov. They enjoy skating with their closest rivals and their challenge to try and overtake them constantly motivates their training.

Irina Lobatcheva & Ilia Averbukh

RUSSIA

FROM RUSSIA, WITH LOVE

"We feel for each other, we understand each other and we support each other."

ILIA

Career Record

Personal

Irina
BORN: February 18, 1973

HEIGHT: 5ft 5in (165cm)

WEIGHT: 110lb (50kg)

Ilia
BORN: December 18, 1973

HEIGHT: 5ft 10in (178cm)

WEIGHT: 143lb (65kg)

Honors

1997 Russian
National Champions

1999 European Bronze Medalists

1999 Grand Prix
Final Bronze Medalists

1999 European Championships, Prague.

Stars of the Past

Historically, figure skating has enjoyed the presence of many uniquely talented and fascinating individuals. There have been champions in the past who have left an indelible mark upon the sport; guiding and developing it through to the mainstream of popular culture. Each of these champions has advanced figure skating in their own self-expressed way.

The likes of Ulrich Salchow, Sonja Henie, Dick Button, Irina Rodnina and Kurt Browning have all progressed the sport through technical achievements; pushing the boundaries to command a greater athletic profile on the ice. Then there were stars such as the Protopopovs, Peggy Fleming, John Curry and Gordeeva and Grinkov, who created such magical performances that the line between sport and art was hardly distinguishable.

Some of our champions have not only promoted the sport out on the ice in competition, but have taken the beauty and intricacy of ice-skating to other media such as film, television and tours. Sonja Henie accomplished one of the greatest records for championship titles and then went on to become one of Hollywood's acclaimed film stars of the 1940s. Many of her films were based around her extraordinary skating talent.

Even today, many of our past stars of the Olympic arena are still performing and contributing as professionals. Brian Boitano has gone on to form his own production company that creates ice-skating specials for television. Even Canada's Barbara Underhill and Paul Martini continued to perform in events, tours and specials for 14 years after they had won their world title and retired from the amateur ranks.

The special quality that is common to all these champions is that they possessed a passion and an energy for figure skating that was fuelled by their own personal goals and aspirations. Each one had a dream that they lived and achieved. It was their achievements that inspired future generations to follow their own dreams.

Jayne Torvill and Christopher Dean.

Ulrich Salchow

Career Record

Personal

BORN: 1877

DIED: 1949

Honors

1901–05 and 1907–10
European Champion

1901–05 and 1907–11
World Champion

1908 Olympic Champion

ULRICH SALCHOW'S NAME HAS BEEN immortalized by the classic jump he invented in 1909 at the height of his career – the Salchow jump. He is the only man in history to win 10 World Championship titles, having already been a silver medalist in 1897, 1899 and 1900 behind the great Austrian skater, Gustav Hugel.

Salchow's most remarkable international competition occurred at the 1902 World Championships held in London. Women had never competed in the Championships at this time, although there was no specified regulation excluding them, and that year Britain's Madge Syers competed, placing second to Salchow. Many felt she should have been awarded the title, and Salchow himself presented her with his gold medal after the Championships.

In 1908, Ulrich won the gold in the Men's event at the first Olympic Games to include figure skating. He competed in his second Olympic Games in 1920 at the age of 42, but was beaten by younger men with greater physical abilities. His reign of the world stage lasted from 1901 through to 1911, excluding the one year he did not compete, 1906. During that time he also won nine European titles. He later became president of the International Skating Union during the difficult years between the two World Wars.

The eponymous Swedish inventor of the classic jump.

Sonja Henie

TO THIS DAY, NO OTHER WOMAN IN the Ladies' singles has equalled the record number of world and Olympic titles achieved by the legendary Norwegian Sonja Henie. Her competitive career brought 10 world and three Olympic titles, all consecutively.

By the age of 10 she was the youngest Norwegian national champion; at 11 she competed in her first Olympic Winter Games; and at 14 she won the first of her world titles. During her reign, she inspired many of the changes taking place in the sport. She shocked the audience and judges at her first Olympics in 1924 by becoming the first woman to include jumping in her free-skating program. She also appeared in a knee-length costume that was considered fairly risqué at the time. It was Henie, too, who introduced the element of dance choreography in her winning performance at the 1928 Olympic Games in St Moritz.

After her retirement from competition in 1936, Sonja Henie went on to become a major box office star in Hollywood, then in the mid-40s she produced and starred in her own professional touring ice show. She had become not only the most successful skater of her time, but also the first skater to make a financially rewarding career as a professional.

Peerless Norwegian champion who dominated the sport between the Wars.

Career Record

Personal

BORN: 1912

DIED: 1969

Honors

1923–36 Norwegian
National Champion

1927–36 World Champion

1928, 1932 and 1936
Olympic Champion

Barbara Ann Scott

Canadian gold medalist admired for the purity and honesty of her skating.

Career Record

Personal

BORN: 1929

Honors

1944–46 and 1948 Canadian
National Champion

1947 and 1948 North American,
European and World Champion

1948 Olympic Champion

BARBARA ANN SCOTT'S FATHER, Lieutenant Clyde Scott, had been a guiding force in her early career, and when he passed away in 1941 she had vowed to herself that one day she would become world and Olympic champion. In 1944 she won the first of four Canadian titles, successfully retaining her crown in 1945 and 1946. In 1947 she not only became the youngest North American champion ever but went on to take the European and World titles as well. Although the European Championships were open to North American skaters at this time, they had never before been won by a North American.

In 1948, she retained all three international titles and crowned her achievements with Olympic gold. To date she is the only Canadian woman to secure an Olympic gold medal in figure skating. Best known for the purity and honesty of her skating, she was a stickler for neatness – a quality that she carried forward in her ability to lay out the compulsory figures.

Today she still attends skating functions and events and is often used as a public speaker to deliver her insights on the sport to today's generations, encouraging others to reach for their goals and commit to their dreams.

Dick Button

Career Record

Personal

BORN: 1929

Honors

1946–52 US National Champion

1947, 1949 and 1951
North American Champion

1948 European Champion

1948–52 World Champion

1948 and 1952 Olympic Champion

Still the youngest Olympic Men's champion in history.

DICK BUTTON'S ACHIEVEMENTS AS AN international competitive figure skater include a host of firsts in addition to those presented to him in the form of gold medals. He was the first skater to perform the double axel, a triple jump (the loop) and a double jump combination (two loops), and it was Button who first performed the spin he invented – the Flying Camel.

In 1948, at the age of 18, Button became the youngest Olympic Men's champion in history, a record that has yet to be broken. He was the first American man to win the World Championships and the first North American to win Olympic gold. During his career, he achieved seven national, three North American, one European, five World and two Olympic titles. He might have added to his single European title had the event not been closed to non-Europeans after his first triumph.

Dick retired from competitive figure skating after his second Olympic title in 1952, performing professionally for a short time before going on to graduate from Harvard Law School. Although it has been almost 50 years since he competed, Button is still very much involved in the sport and can be found at most major international events. He has become America's primary sports commentator and spokesperson for the sport.

Peggy Fleming

Career Record

Personal

BORN: 1948

Honors

1964–68 US National Champion

1966–68 World Champion

1968 Olympic Champion

WHEN THEIR ENTIRE TEAM DIED IN A plane crash on the way to the World Championships in 1961, people predicted that it would be many years before the US could find the talent to replace the skaters they had lost. However, Peggy Fleming was already on her way, and in 1964 she won the first of five consecutive national titles, following with eighth place in her first Olympic Winter Games. A year later, she took the bronze medal at her second World Championships, and in 1966 became champion, continuing her reign through to 1968.

Winning America's only gold medal at the 1968 Olympics in Grenoble elevated Peggy to superstar status, as a result of the television broadcast and commentary. After retirement from amateur competition following her success of 1968, Peggy went on to star in several television specials and toured with various ice shows.

Still very connected to high-profile figure skating, Peggy is a sports commentator for the American Broadcasting Company, and, having successfully battled with breast cancer in early 1998, has also become a highly regarded spokesperson about breast cancer.

A skater of beauty and grace.

Ludmila Belousova
& Oleg Protopopov

A husband and wife team of remarkable precision and timing.

TO THIS DAY THE HUSBAND AND WIFE team of Ludmila Belousova and Oleg Protopopov are renowned for their rarely matched sense of unison and elegance. Both Ludmila and Oleg started skating relatively late in life, and when they teamed up as a pair in 1954, aged 19 and 22, no Soviet coach wished to work with them as they were considered too old.

Left to their own devices, Ludmila and Oleg went on to develop a style that can best be described as pure ballet on ice. They had an extraordinary slowness when completing very difficult moves that gave an appearance of effortlessness never seen before. At that time the top pairs were performing the death spiral on a backward outside edge, but Ludmila's great depth of edge and balance, together with Oleg's vast strength, allowed them to enhance this move and perform it on the more difficult inside edge.

They married in 1957, became Olympic champions in 1964 and 1968, and in addition were the European and world champions through an entire Olympiad. Ludmila was 36 and Oleg 33 when they took their second Olympic gold, confirming their place as one of the most famous teams the world has ever known. They defected to Switzerland in 1979, while touring with a Russian ice show, and continued to perform and compete professionally until 1992.

Career Record

Personal

BORN: Belousova 1932

Protopopov 1935

Honors

1964 and 1968 Olympic Champions

1965–68 European Champions

1965–68 World Champions

93

Diane Towler
& Bernard Ford

Career Record

Personal

BORN: Towler 1948
Ford 1948

Honors

1965–68 British Champions
1966–69 European Champions
1966–69 World Champions

Towler and Ford attracted new followers to ice dance with their lively and innovative approach.

DIANE TOWLER AND BERNARD FORD entered the international ice dance scene in 1964 at the World Championships in Dortmund. A young couple, both 16, they came 13th in a field of 16, but only a year later they rose to fourth in the world. Then in 1966 they took both the European and world titles, and dominated the world of ice dance for the next three years, winning every major championship they entered. Unfortunately ice dance was not considered athletically challenging enough to be included in the Olympic Winter Games of 1968.

Diane and Bernard played a significant part in changing the world's perception of their discipline. They had the ability to skate deep edges as never before, while their speed, together with an uncanny sense of synchronization, provided a new element of excitement to ice dance. These elements, coupled with the livelier music and costumes that they used, added a new interest for the followers of ice dance, and the discipline enjoyed an increase in its number of spectators.

Today, both Diane and Bernard have gone on to become well-known coaches in the sport, Bernard as director of a center in Seattle, Washington, and Diane teaching at a rink in London.

STARS OF THE PAST

Liudmila Pakhomova & Alexandr Gorshkov

Career Record

Personal

BORN: Pakhomova 1947
Gorshkov 1950

Honors

1969–76 Russian
National Champions

1970–71 and 1973–76
European Champions

1970–74 and 1976
World Champions

1976 Olympic Champions

Pakhomova and Gorshkov started the Russian dominance of ice dance.

THE START OF RUSSIA'S DOMINANCE OF the ice dance discipline began in 1970, when Liudmila Pakhomova and Alexandr Gorshkov became the first Soviet dance couple to win a world title. Of the 19 World Championships held since then, only six have been won by non-Soviet or non-Russian couples.

Pakhomova and Gorshkov became almost unbeatable. In the six years following their first win in 1970, they lost the European title only once – to the West German brother-and-sister team Angelika and Erich Buck – and won every world title except in 1975, when they did not compete. In 1976, in the first-ever ice dance event of the Olympic Winter Games, they returned from their year out to take the Olympic title, followed by their sixth World Championship.

Their unique blend of Russian ballet, together with American and English ballroom characteristics, made Pakhomova and Gorshkov innovators of their time. Even today, their style is still featured by the Russian ice dancers at the elite end of the sport. In 1974, Liudmila and Alexandr left another legacy to the sport when, together with their coach, Elena Tchaikovskaya, they created the Tango Romantica. Today this dance is one of the official ISU compulsory dances for competitions and championships all over the world.

John Curry

Career Record

Personal

BORN: 1949

DIED: 1994

Honors

1971, 1973–76 British
National Champion

1976 European Champion

1976 World Champion

1976 Olympic Champion

John Curry brought the art and creativity of the ballet world on to the ice.

JOHN CURRY'S LEGACY TO SKATING WAS his ability to transfer the art and creativity of the ballet world on to the ice. He was the consummate classical dancer, with a great style and line that also made him a formidable technician. He began skating at the age of seven only because it was the closest thing to ballet – a discipline his father had refused to let him learn.

Although his international career started in 1970, it wasn't until John came under the guidance of well-respected Italian coach Carlo Fassi that he earned his first international medal, a bronze, at the 1974 European Championships. Two years later, with five national titles to his name, John Curry went on to a hat-trick, winning the 1976 European, World and Olympic titles.

After his amateur career had finished, John developed the first ice show to be performed in theaters with ice laid down on Broadway stages. He was the star of as well as the artistic genius behind his own company's productions.

Sadly, John died in 1994 from complications resulting from Aids, but he has left his legacy to the sport. His passion and expression for artistic skating have influenced the developing styles of later generations.

Irina Rodnina & Alexei Ulanov/Alexandr Zaitsev

Career Record

Personal

BORN: Rodnina 1949

Ulanov 1948

Zaitsev 1951

Honors

1969–72 World Champion
with Ulanov

1973–78 World Champion
with Zaitsev

1972 Olympic Champion
with Ulanov

1976 and 1980 Olympic
Champion with Zaitsev

ONLY THE LEGENDARY SONJA HENIE has won as many world and Olympic medals as the Soviet pairs dynamo Irina Rodnina, who achieved her record with two different partners. The first of Irina's partnerships was with Alexei Ulanov, with whom she won four consecutive world and one Olympic gold. Rodnina and Ulanov took pair skating from the elegance and balletic style of the Protopopovs to a new level of dynamic speed and athletic energy. Using jumps, lifts and loud music, they entered the international scene like a bolt of lightning to take their first world title in 1969.

Irina and Alexei had a dramatic split following their Olympic title in 1972, when Alexei fell in love with Ludmila Smirnova, one of a rival Soviet pair. Irina was said to have been in love with Ulanov herself, so the split was especially emotional for her.

Alexandr Zaitsev, two years her junior, was Irina's second hand-picked partner. With Zaitsev, she carried on where she had left off by winning the 1973 World Championships in Bratislava, then adding five more world titles and two Olympic golds. The pair married in 1975 and the birth of their son in 1979 took Irina out of competitive skating for a while. However, they returned to win a second gold medal at the 1980 Olympic Winter Games at Lake Placid. Now divorced, they both live and coach in the US.

Irina Rodnina skates on with her second partner, Alexandr Zaitsev.

97

Robin Cousins

Figure skating's Renaissance Man.

he quickly excelled on the ice so that, only six years after he began skating, he found himself at the top of the Junior British Championships podium. At the Senior Nationals in 1974 he came second behind the future Olympic champion John Curry, and when John won his Olympic title in 1976, Robin was already ranked in the world top 10. Moving to Colorado Springs to train with Carlo and Christa Fassi, Robin progressed quickly to take the world silver medal in 1979 before striking gold in 1980 at both the European Championships and Olympic Winter Games.

Although he has achieved the highest honors of elite sport, the Olympic gold is just the tip of the iceberg for this man. He has tackled leading roles on the West End stage, he has recorded various works (including an Andrew Lloyd Webber compilation), he is a sports commentator for the BBC and he has produced and choreographed various tours, television specials and Hollywood movies. He could be classified as figure skating's Renaissance Man.

Career Record

Personal

BORN: 1957

Honors

1976–79 British National Champion

1979 and 1980 World Silver Medalist

1980 European Champion

1980 Olympic Champion

FROM A VERY EARLY AGE ROBIN COUSINS was attracted to the world of music and dance, taking ballet lessons from the age of seven and showing great promise as a dancer. However, his love of jumping and sailing through the air soon directed his attention towards figure skating.

With extraordinary balance and rhythm,

Scott Hamilton

A man of unquenchable spirit and a skater of champion quality.

Career Record

Personal

BORN: 1958

Honors

1981–84 US National Champion
1981–84 World Champion
1984 Olympic Champion

ONE OF THE MOST INSPIRATIONAL STARS OF figure skating, Scott Hamilton has faced obstacles throughout his life that would have deterred many a lesser spirit. As a toddler he was diagnosed with Schwachman's syndrome, a rare intestinal disease that prevents the body from absorbing nutrients and seriously hinders growth. Throughout childhood he received intensive medical treatment and was attached to a permanent feeding tube.

Despite all this, Scott took to the ice at the age of nine, and soon afterwards his growth development improved. Although he had made a miraculous recovery from his childhood disease, many people felt he was too small and frail for a champion ice skater. But Scott was stronger than he looked.

In 1978 his mother, who had supported him throughout his childhood illness, died of cancer, and Scott, devastated, seriously considered leaving the sport. However, a change of coach and training environment provided the boost that he needed, and in 1981 he won the US title. He went on to win the world title the same year and retained both these titles for the next three years. His amateur career culminated with Olympic Gold at the 1984 Games in Sarajevo, and as a professional he went on to become one of the greatest performers of the twentieth century, despite having to overcome testicular cancer in 1996.

99

Barbara Underhill
& Paul Martini

BARBARA UNDERHILL AND PAUL MARTINI'S gold medal at the 1984 World Championships in Ottawa came less than three weeks after a disastrous performance at the 1984 Olympics, where they had been contenders for the title. So poorly had they performed at the Olympics that their coach, Louis Strong, had doubted whether they should even compete in Ottawa at all. As it was, the world title was all the sweeter for coming in front of their home crowd – and in winning it they had beaten the newly crowned Olympic Champions, Elena Valova and Oleg Vasiliev of Russia.

Underhill and Martini began skating together in 1975, when Barbara was 13 and Paul 15. In 1979 they won their first of five consecutive Canadian titles, although in the five years as Canada's best, they won only two world medals.

It was following retirement from amateur competition directly after the 1984 World Championships that Underhill and Martini

developed into one of the most revered partnerships of pair skating. They won seven World Professional Championships and performed some of the sport's most memorable pieces.

When they decided to dissolve their partnership in 1998, they performed a gala entitled "One Last Time" to reflect the two decades they had skated together.

The revered Canadian partnership who graced the sport as amateurs and professionals.

Career Record

Personal

BORN: Underhill 1962

Martini 1960

Honors

1979–83 Canadian
National Champions

1984 World Champions

100

Jayne Torvill
& Christopher Dean

JAYNE TORVILL AND CHRISTOPHER DEAN have constantly challenged the limits of ice dancing, becoming known as the greatest ice dancers of all time. Chris was always the creative force behind the partnership, while Jayne was the technician. It was a perfect partnership that began in 1975.

After taking fifth place in their first Olympic Winter Games in 1980, they began to train full-time with Betty Callaway, and next season became the new European and world champions. Other than in 1983, when they were not able to compete at the European Championships, they continued to dominate these events until 1984.

Each year they would come out with an innovative program that changed the face of

Ravel's "Bolero" at the 1984 Olympics was the perfect performance.

Career Record

Personal

BORN: Torvill 1957

Dean 1958

Honors

1981–1984 & 1994
British Champions

1981–1982, 1984 & 1994
European Champions

1981–1984 World Champions

1984 Olympic Champions

ice dance. Their 1984 program to Ravel's "Bolero" won them the Olympic title and earned them straight 6.0s for artistic merit. No other skaters in any discipline of figure skating have earned as many perfect scores as Torvill and Dean.

After winning the Olympic gold and recapturing their world title in 1984, Torvill and Dean retired from amateur competition and enjoyed a very successful and lucrative professional career for the next ten years. They returned to the amateur stage in 1994, competing against some couples half their age, to take the national and European titles, but – controversially – only the bronze at the Lillehammer Olympics.

Katarina Witt GERMANY

It was Katarina Witt's "Carmen" that triumphed at the 1988 Olympics.

KATARINA WITT IS THE ONLY WOMAN SINCE Sonja Henie to win two Olympic gold medals in Ladies' singles, and the only woman to match Henie's record of six consecutive European titles.

Four years after starting on the ice aged five, she was selected as a potential talent and assigned to the top East German figure skating coach Jutta Muller. Katarina was already executing triple salchows by the age of 11, and when she competed at her first World Championships three years later she made the top 10.

In 1984, Witt won the first of her four world titles and, apart from 1986 when she was beaten by the American skater Debi Thomas, Witt was world champion for the complete Olympiad between 1984 and 1988. She and Thomas met again at the 1988 Olympics in Calgary, where both skaters arrived with free programs to the music of "Carmen". This time it was Witt who triumphed, leaving Thomas with the bronze behind Elizabeth Manley.

Katarina won her last world title one month later and then retired from eligible skating. Although she was reinstated in 1994 to compete for Germany at the Lillehammer Games, the technical requirements of the sport had advanced so much in her absence that she could manage only sixth place. The winner of the event, Oksana Baiul was almost half Katarina's age.

Brian Boitano

ONE OF THE REMARKABLE FEATURES OF Brian Boitano's amateur skating career is the fact that he remained at the same training rink and with the same coach, Linda Leaver, from his first steps on to the ice through to an Olympic gold medal.

His greatest passion on the ice was for the jumping, and that strength was one of his trademark qualities.

Boitano developed quickly, becoming US Junior National champion in 1978, although the senior title was more elusive. Brian arrived on the scene at the height of Scott Hamilton's career and had to wait in the shadows until Hamilton retired in 1984. The next year, Brian took the first of four consecutive US National Championships.

He added the 1986 World Championships in Switzerland and, despite losing his world crown the next year to Brian Orser, he began to set his sights on Olympic gold. At Calgary in 1988, dressed in a military-style costume, he skated to the soundtrack from the film *Napoleon*. It provided the edge Brian needed to take the gold, and a month later he also took back the world title from Orser.

Boitano retired after that to pursue a professional career, and although he was reinstated for the 1994 Olympic Games, he could manage only sixth place. He had already achieved every skater's dream of Olympic gold.

Career Record

Personal

BORN: 1963

Honors

1985–88 US National Champion
1986 and 1988 World Champion
1988 Olympic Champion

A skater of great power, Brian Boitano won Gold at the 1988 Olympics.

103

Ekaterina Gordeeva & Sergei Grinkov

G and G – one of the great love stories of all time.

IT WAS A PARTNERSHIP THAT STARTED WITH two young teenagers and developed into one of the greatest pair teams and love stories of all time. Known in skating circles as G and G, Ekaterina Gordeeva and Sergei Grinkov were Soviet heroes who astounded the world with their power and grace on the ice.

The Central Red Army Club in Moscow is where both Ekaterina and Sergei first began skating as pre-schoolers. Neither showing the ability to become great single skaters, they were groomed for pairs and were teamed together in 1982 when Ekaterina was 11 and Sergei 15. The partnership immediately flourished and within less than a year they became the 1984 World Junior Champions.

Before G and G, there had been the sublime elegance and synchronization of Liudmila Belousova and Oleg Protopopov in the sixties. Then trends changed in the sev-

enties and the world was amazed by the speed and immense athleticism of Irina Rodnina and her partners Alexei Ulanov and Alexandr Zaitsev. Gordeeva and Grinkov brought a new style of pair skating to the eighties that the world had never experienced before. Here was a pair that combined the traditions of Russian ballet with some of the most dynamic athletic feats the sport had ever witnessed. This combination of grace and power brought a new dimension to pairs skating.

In their amateur career, G and G went on to win four European and world titles with two Olympic golds. Their final European and Olympic titles of 1994 occurred after a four-year absence from eligible competition, during which they married in 1991 and their daughter Daria was born in 1992. After a complete new generation of Olympians had

emerged, G and G were able to come back and recapture sport's highest accolade. Their union off the ice had brought an element of intimacy to their performances that showed the depth of their love for one another.

Tragically, while practicing in Lake Placid on November 20, 1995, Sergei died of a massive heart attack in young Ekaterina's arms. The world had lost one of its greatest male pair skaters; young Ekaterina had lost the love of her life and the father of her child. Ekaterina skated solo for the first time in a specially organized tribute to her late husband the following year. The program was haunting and yet magical at the same time and sparked Ekaterina's love for skating again. She returned to the ice as a single skater and began a new career competing and touring on her own. She says that although Sergei is not actually out there holding her hand any longer, his spirit helps to carry her through into a new dimension of skating.

Career Record
Personal

BORN: Gordeeva 1971
Grinkov 1967
DIED: Grinkov 1995

Honors

1987–1988, 1990 & 1994 European Champions

1986–1987 & 1989–1990 World Champions

1988 and 1994 Olympic Champions

Kurt Browning

One of the best skaters never to win an Olympic medal.

Career Record

Personal

BORN: 1966

Honors

1989–1991 and 1993 Canadian Champion

1989–1991 and 1993 World Champion

FROM A NATION THAT IS FAMOUS FOR ITS skating celebrities, Kurt Browning is perhaps the greatest skating star Canada has ever produced. He is the only Canadian man to win four world championship titles and bring advancements to the sport both artistically and athletically.

Raised in a small Canadian ranching town, Kurt began skating at the age of three. That winter his father Dewey transformed their front yard into a skating rink. Initially drawn to ice hockey, Kurt began figure skating only as a means of enhancing his hockey skills. It wasn't long before his jumping ability and quick intricate blade work had him

training as a full time figure skater. By 1983, he was the Canadian Novice Champion and only two years later he moved up to become the Junior Champion.

Through 1987 and 1988, Kurt skated in the shadows of fellow great Canadian Brian Orser. Orser was the 1987 World Champion and took the silver medal at the 1988 Calgary Olympics. Kurt made his first real impact on the world stage at Orser's last amateur World Championships in 1988. Kurt didn't make the winner's podium there, but he did make the *Guinness Book of Records* for becoming the first skater ever to land a quadruple jump in competition. Brian Orser

retired after the 1988 season and the following year Kurt took the first of his four Canadian Men's titles.

After the 1989 Canadian title, Kurt went on to win the World Championships that year in Paris. He reigned as world champion for the next three years, losing to the Ukrainian Viktor Petrenko in 1992, but recapturing the title in 1993.

Although Browning dominated men's figure skating during the late eighties and early nineties, Olympic glory always eluded him. He competed in three Olympic Winter Games – 1988, 1992 and 1994 – but never took a medal at any of these events. He was the favorite for the Albertville Games of 1992, but a back injury prior to the Games affected his performance and he could only manage sixth place.

He is probably one of the best skaters never to win an Olympic medal.

Kurt retired after the 1994 Games and went on to become one of the most challenging professionals on the circuit. He has created some of the most memorable programs and continues to push the artistic boundaries of the sport. To this day, in respect of both his athleticism and his creativity, Kurt Browning is a true innovator of the sport.

105

Kristi Yamaguchi

Career Record

Personal

Born: 1971

Honors

1989–1990 US National Champion
(Pairs)

1991–1992 World Champion

1992 US National Champion
(Singles)

1992 Olympic Champion

WHEN AMERICAN DOROTHY HAMILL WON the gold medal at the 1976 Olympic Winter Games in Innsbruck, Kristi Yamaguchi was just five years old. Hamill's performance in Innsbruck inspired the young fourth-generation American of Japanese descent to take up figure skating. The Yamaguchi family would never have thought back then that 16 years later their young daughter would follow in Hamill's footsteps to become only the fifth American woman to win the Ladies' singles Olympic gold.

Kristi was not known only for her talent as a singles skater. From 1983 through to 1990 she skated pairs with Rudi Galindo. The partnership enjoyed huge success, becoming the 1988 World Junior Champions the same year Kristi won the respective Ladies' event. Yamaguchi and Galindo went on to become the US National Pairs Champions in 1989 and 1990, culminating in a fifth-place finish at the World Championships of 1990. Kristi was ranked fourth that same year in the Ladies' singles.

After 1990, to Galindo's great disappointment, Kristi took the advice of her support group and decided to leave pairs skating to concentrate on her singles career. Although upsetting for all involved, the decision proved to be highly successful for Kristi. The following year she won the gold in the World Championships in an American sweep, with teammates Tonya Harding and Nancy Kerrigan taking silver and bronze respectively.

The 1992 Olympic Winter Games in Albertville saw Kristi fend off the Japanese jumping phenomenon Midori Ito to take the Olympic title. Ito was the first woman in the history of the sport to land a triple axel, at the 1989 World Championships in Paris. Kristi went on one month after the Games to win her second World Championships and then retired from the amateur rankings.

Today Kristi is one of the headliners of the hugely successful "Stars on Ice" tour. She is known as one of the world's most popular professional skaters, winning many of the major pro championships. She is heavily involved in charities for children and women and has become one of the top spokespersons for her sport.

Kristi Yamaguchi wins Gold at Albertville in 1992.

Nancy Kerrigan

UNITED STATES OF AMERICA

A skater of great poise and grace and a woman of courage and determination.

BY THOSE IN THE KNOW IN THE SKATING world, Nancy Kerrigan is recognized for her strong technical components matched with a lyrical and elegant style of skating. To non-followers of the sport, though, she is best remembered for being involved in one of the most sensational sporting scandals of Olympic history.

It was at the 1994 US Nationals, where Kerrigan was favorite to retain her title from the previous year. Coming off an official practice session at these Championships she was attacked and struck across her right knee by an unknown assailant wielding a steel bar. Instantly the story flashed around the entire world. A media frenzy followed the sport to the ensuing Olympic Winter Games in Lillehammer.

At first Kerrigan was unsure as to whether she would be able to skate again, but a miraculous recovery aided by Nancy's sheer determination saw her take a place on the US Olympic team. At the Games she narrowly missed gold by one-tenth of a point to the Ukrainian skating sensation Oksana Baiul. But the courage and determination Kerrigan demonstrated in coming back from her attack made her an overnight celebrity.

Along with the Olympic silver medal in 1994, Kerrigan was Olympic bronze medalist at the 1992 Games and took a bronze medal at the 1991 World Championships before moving up to the silver position in 1992. Her battle with competition nerves saw her fall from the podium in 1993 to fifth place, but she worked diligently and sought the assistance of a sports psychologist that saw her through to her outstanding performances at the 1994 Games.

Nancy retired from eligible status directly following Lillehammer. She did not go on to compete at the World Championships one month later. In 1995, Nancy married her agent Jerry Solomon and their first child, a boy named Matthew, was born in December 1996. Although she still performs as a professional today, her new positions as a wife and mother are her top priority.

Career Record

Personal

BORN: 1969

Honors

1992 World Silver Medalist

1994 Olympic Silver Medalist

1993 US National Champion

107

Oksana Baiul

Oksana Baiul wins Olympic Gold at Lillehammer in 1994.

Bonaly. Two months later, at the World Championships in Prague, she moved further up the podium to become the youngest champion since Sonja Henie back in 1927; Oksana was 15.

The following year at the Olympic Games in Lillehammer, Oksana went on to win the title, narrowly beating Nancy Kerrigan. Again it was her sheer strength of character that took Oksana through to glory; at the Games she competed with three stitches in her leg and a back injury caused by a collision.

Upon reaching sport's highest achievement, Oksana retired from eligible skating at an age when many other skaters were just starting their quest for Olympic glory. Like many teenage sports sensations, Oksana faced a trying time living with her instant celebrity status and had a bout with alcohol abuse during 1997.

She sought help with her problems and then returned in force as a professional skater, touring with various shows and competing in pro events. Her hope is that she may one day be able to return to her form of 1994 and compete again at an Olympic Games.

THE ROAD TO OKSANA BAIUL'S OLYMPIC gold medal in 1994 is one of the most touching stories of triumph over tragedy.

Often described as the orphan of the skating world, Oksana's childhood was filled with heartbreak. When she was just two years old her father walked out on Oksana and her mother, Marina. Oksana's grandfather became a guiding force in her initial skating endeavors. Sadly, the grandfather passed away in 1987, followed by Oksana's grandmother in 1988. Then, when Oksana was 13, her mother died suddenly of ovarian cancer and Oksana had only her coach at the time, Stanislav Korytek, as a means of support. But only a year after her mother's death Korytek left to go and coach in Canada.

At first Oksana threw her skates away,

but she soon realized that without skating there was a void that emphasised her isolation. She approached top Ukrainian coach Galina Zmievskaya, who had taken Viktor Petrenko to Olympic gold in 1992. Zmievskaya had already decided to retire from coaching after the success of Petrenko, but upon seeing Oksana on the ice she immediately changed her mind. She took Oksana under her wing and Viktor Petrenko assisted with the training expenses. Both Zmievskaya and Petrenko knew they were looking at a potential Olympic Champion.

Oksana blazed onto the international scene like a comet coming from nowhere. She entered the European Championships in 1993 as the Ukrainian Champion and took the silver medal behind France's Surya

Career Record

Personal

BORN: 1978

Honors

1993–1994 Ukrainian National Champion

1993 World Champion

1994 Olympic Champion

Oksana "Pasha" Grishuk & Evgeny Platov

Career Record

Personal

BORN: 1972 and 1967

Honors

1996–1998 Russian National Champions

1996–1997 European Champions

1996–1998 Champion Series Final Champions

1994–1997 World Champions

1994 and 1998 Olympic Champions

The unconquerable Russian ice-dance partnership of the late 1990s.

RUSSIA HAS DOMINATED ICE DANCE SINCE the event was included in the Olympic Winter Games back in 1976. It was at about that time that a five-year old Oksana Grishuk was taking her first steps onto the ice in her home town of Odessa near the Black Sea. Also at this time nine-year-old Evgeny Platov was returning to the sport at the prestigious Army Club in Moscow after an absence of several years.

Both Grishuk and Platov enjoyed international success with former partners at the World Junior Championships; Evgeny won the title from 1984 to 1986 with Elena Krikanova and then Oksana took the title in 1988 with Alexandr Chichkov. But the Soviet system did not think either of these initial partnerships would win Olympic medals so they brought together the stronger components of each.

It was not long before Grishuk and Platov took their place at the top of world ice dancing. At their first World Championships together, in 1990, they finished fifth and thereafter moved up one place each year until they took the title for the first time in 1994. It was also in 1994 that Oksana and Evgeny competed in one of the most extraordinary ice dance events of Olympic history. The 1994 Olympic Games in Norway saw the return of ice dance legends Jayne Torvill and Christopher Dean, the 1984 Olympic Champions. Torvill and Dean had narrowly beaten Grishuk and Platov at the European Championships just weeks before the Games were to commence. Then, at the Games, Grishuk and Platov turned the tables to come from third place after the original dance to take the Olympic title.

The next four years saw Grishuk and Platov unconquerable. They won every major championship they entered, but personal conflict and a knee injury saw the partnership face difficult times. During much of the 1996–1997 season there was even speculation as to whether the partnership could weather the storms and continue to the 1998 Olympic Games. Ever the professionals, Evgeny and Oksana, who altered her name to Pasha in late 1997, changed coaches and progressed through to take their second Olympic gold in Nagano.

It was only six months after retiring from eligible competition following the 1998 Games that Grishuk and Platov split up and moved to take new partnerships; Pasha with Alexandr Zhulin and Evgeny with Zhulin's former partner and ex-wife Maia Usova. Grishuk and Zhulin skated together for less than a year, but Platov and Usova went on to become world professional ice dance champions in 1999. Pasha has recently decided to try her hand at singles skating while she pursues her acting career in Los Angeles.

Ice Champions

WINTER OLYMPIC GAMES

MEN

1908	London	Ulrich Salchow, Sweden
1920	Antwerp	Gillis Grafstom, Sweden
1924	Chamonix	Gillis Grafstom, Sweden
1928	St Moritz	Gillis Grafstom, Sweden
1932	Lake Placid	Karl Schafer, Austria
1936	Garmisch	Karl Schafer, Austria
1948	St Moritz	Richard Button, United States of America
1952	Oslo	Richard Button, United States of America
1956	Cortina	Hayes Alan Jenkins, United States of America
1960	Squaw Valley	David Jenkins, United States of America
1964	Innsbruck	Manfred Schnelldorfer, West Germany
1968	Grenoble	Wolfgang Schwarz, Austria
1972	Sapporo	Ondrej Nepela, Czechoslovakia
1976	Innsbruck	John Curry, Great Britain
1980	Lake Placid	Robin Cousins, Great Britain
1984	Sarajevo	Scott Hamilton, United States of America
1988	Calgary	Brian Boitano, United States of America
1992	Albertville	Viktor Petrenko, Unified team
1994	Lillehammer	Alexei Urmanov, Russia
1998	Nagano	Ilya Kulik, Russia

WOMEN

1908	London	Madge Syers, Great Britain
1920	Antwerp	Magda Julin-Mauroy, Sweden
1924	Chamonix	Herma Plank-Szabo, Austria
1928	St Moritz	Sonja Henie, Norway
1932	Lake Placid	Sonja Henie, Norway
1936	Garmisch	Sonja Henie, Norway
1948	St Moritz	Barbara Ann Scott, Canada
1952	Oslo	Jeannette Altwegg, Great Britain
1956	Cortina	Tenley Albright, United States of America
1960	Squaw Valley	Carol Heiss, United States of America
1964	Innsbruck	Sjoukje Dijkstra, The Netherlands
1968	Grenoble	Peggy Fleming, United States of America
1972	Sapporo	Beatrix Schuba, Austria
1976	Innsbruck	Dorothy Hamill, United States of America
1980	Lake Placid	Anett Putzsch, East Germany
1984	Sarajevo	Katarina Witt, East Germany
1988	Calgary	Katarina Witt, East Germany
1992	Albertville	Kristi Yamaguchi, United States of America
1994	Lillehammer	Oksana Baiul, Ukraine
1998	Nagano	Tara Lipinski, United States

PAIRS

1908	London	Anna Hubler & Heinrich Burger, Germany
1920	Antwerp	Ludowika Jakobsson & Walter Jakobsson, Finland
1924	Chamonix	Helene Engelmann & Alfred Berger, Austria
1928	St Moritz	Andree Brunet & Pierre Brunet, France
1932	Lake Placid	Andree Brunet & Pierre Brunet, France
1936	Garmisch	Maxie Herber & Ernst Baier, Germany
1948	St Moritz	Micheline Lannoy & Pierre Baugniet, Belgium
1952	Oslo	Ria Falk & Paul West, West Germany
1956	Cortina	Elizabeth Schwarz & Kurt Oppelt, Austria
1960	Squaw Valley	Barbara Wager & Robert Paul, Canada
1964	Innsbruck	Ludmila Belousova & Oleg Protopopov, Soviet Union
1968	Grenoble	Ludmila Belousova & Oleg Protopopov, Soviet Union
1972	Sapporo	Irina Rodnina & Alexei Ulanov, Soviet Union
1976	Innsbruck	Irina Rodnina & Alexandr Zaitsev, Soviet Union
1980	Lake Placid	Irina Rodnina & Alexandr Zaitsev, Soviet Union
1984	Sarajevo	Elena Valova & Oleg Vassiliev, Soviet Union
1988	Calgary	Ekaterina Gordeeva & Sergei Grinkov, Soviet Union
1992	Albertville	Natalia Mishketenok & Artur Dmitriev, Unified Team
1994	Lillehammer	Ekaterina Gordeeva & Sergei Grinkov, Russia
1998	Nagano	Oksana Kazakova & Artur Dmitriev, Russia

ICE DANCING

1976	Innsbruck	Liudmila Pakhomova & Aleksandr Gorshkov, Soviet Union
1980	Lake Placid	Gennadi Karponosov & Natalia Linichuk, Soviet Union
1984	Sarajevo	Jayne Torvill & Christopher Dean, Great Britain
1988	Calgary	Natalia Bestemianova & Andrei Bukin, Soviet Union
1992	Albertville	Marina Klimova & Sergei Ponomarenko, Unified Team
1994	Lillehammer	Oksana Grishuk & Evgeny Platov, Russia
1998	Nagano	Oksana Grishuk & Evgeny Platov, Russia

WORLD CHAMPIONSHIPS

MEN

1896	St Petersburg	Gilbert Fuchs, Germany
1897	Stockholm	Gustav Hugel, Austria
1898	London	Henning Grenander, Sweden
1899	Davos	Gustav Hugel, Austria
1900	Davos	Gustav Hugel, Austria
1901	Stockholm	Ulrich Salchow, Sweden
1902	London	Ulrich Salchow, Sweden
1903	St Petersburg	Ulrich Salchow, Sweden
1904	Berlin	Ulrich Salchow, Sweden
1905	Stockholm	Ulrich Salchow, Sweden
1906	Munich	Gilbert Fuchs, Germany
1907	Vienna	Ulrich Salchow, Sweden
1908	Troppau	Ulrich Salchow, Sweden
1909	Stockholm	Ulrich Salchow, Sweden
1910	Davos	Ulrich Salchow, Sweden
1911	Berlin	Ulrich Salchow, Sweden
1912	Manchester	Fritz Kachler, Austria
1913	Vienna	Fritz Kachler, Austria
1914	Helsinki	Gosta Sandahl, Sweden
1922	Stockholm	Gillis Grafstrom, Sweden
1923	Vienna	Fritz Kachler, Austria
1924	Manchester	Gillis Grafstrom, Sweden
1925	Vienna	Willy Bockl, Austria
1926	Berlin	Willy Bockl, Austria
1927	Davos	Willy Bockl, Austria
1928	Berlin	Willy Bockl, Austria
1929	London	Gillis Grafstrom, Sweden
1930	New York	Karl Schafer, Austria
1931	Berlin	Karl Schafer, Austria
1932	Montreal	Karl Schafer, Austria
1933	Zurich	Karl Schafer, Austria
1934	Stockholm	Karl Schafer, Austria
1935	Budapest	Karl Schafer, Austria
1936	Paris	Karl Schafer, Austria
1937	Vienna	Felix Kaspar, Austria
1938	Berlin	Felix Kaspar, Austria
1939	Budapest	Graham Sharp, Great Britain
1947	Stockholm	Hans Gerscwiler, Switzerland
1948	Davos	Richard Button, United States of America
1949	Paris	Richard Button, United States of America

1950	London	Richard Button, United States of America
1951	Milan	Richard Button, United States of America
1952	Paris	Richard Button, United States of America
1953	Davos	Hayes A Jenkins, United States of America
1954	Oslo	Hayes A Jenkins, United States of America
1955	Vienna	Hayes A Jenkins, United States of America
1956	Garmisch	Hayes A Jenkins, United States of America
1957	Colo Springs	David Jenkins, United States of America
1958	Paris	David Jenkins, United States of America
1959	Colo Springs	David Jenkins, United States of America
1960	Vancouver	Alain Giletti, France
1961	No championships held	
1962	Prague	Donald Jackson, Canada
1963	Cortina	Donald McPherson, Canada
1964	Dortmund	Manfred Schnelldorfer, West Germany
1965	Colo Springs	Alain Calmat, France
1966	Davos	Emmerich Danzer, Austria
1967	Vienna	Emmerich Danzer, Austria
1968	Geneva	Emmerich Danzer, Austria
1969	Colo Springs	Tim Wood, United States of America
1970	Ljubjana	Tim Wood, United States of America
1971	Lyon	Ondrej Nepela, Czechoslovakia
1972	Calgary	Ondrej Nepela, Czechoslovakia
1973	Bratislava	Ondrej Nepela, Czechoslovakia
1974	Munich	Jan Hoffmann, East Germany
1975	Colo Springs	Sergei Volkov, Soviet Union
1976	Gothenburg	John Curry, Great Britain
1977	Tokyo	Vladimir Kovalev, Soviet Union
1978	Ottawa	Charles Tickner, United States of America
1979	Vienna	Vladimir Kovalev, Soviet Union
1980	Dortmund	Jan Hoffmann, East Germany
1981	Hartford	Scott Hamilton, United States of America
1982	Copenhagen	Scott Hamilton, United States of America
1983	Helsinki	Scott Hamilton, United States of America
1984	Ottawa	Scott Hamilton, United States of America
1985	Tokyo	Alexandr Fadeev, Soviet Union
1986	Geneva	Brian Boitano, United States of America
1987	Cincinnati	Brian Orser, Canada
1988	Budapest	Brian Boitano, United States of America
1989	Paris	Kurt Browning, Canada
1990	Halifax	Kurt Browning, Canada
1991	Munich	Kurt Browning, Canada
1992	Oakland	Viktor Petrenko, Soviet Union
1993	Prague	Kurt Browning, Canada
1994	Chiba	Elvis Stojko, Canada
1995	Birmingham	Elvis Stojko, Canada
1996	Edmonton	Todd Eldredge, United States of America
1997	Lausanne	Elvis Stojko, Canada
1998	Minneapolis	Aleksei Yagudin, Russia
1999	Helsinki	Aleksei Yagudin, Russia

WOMEN

1906	Munich	Madge Syers, Great Britain
1907	Vienna	Madge Syers, Great Britain
1908	Troppau	Lily Kronberger, Hungary
1909	Stockholm	Lily Kronberger, Hungary
1910	Davos	Lily Kronberger, Hungary
1911	Berlin	Lily Kronberger, Hungary
1912	Manchester	Opika von Horvath, Hungary
1913	Vienna	Opika von Horvath, Hungary
1914	Helsinki	Opika von Horvath, Hungary
1922	Stockholm	Herma Plank-Szabo, Austria
1923	Vienna	Herma Plank-Szabo, Austria
1924	Manchester	Herma Plank-Szabo, Austria
1925	Vienna	Herma Jaross-Szabo, Austria
1926	Berlin	Herma Jaross-Szabo, Austria
1927	Davos	Sonja Henie, Norway
1928	Berlin	Sonja Henie, Norway
1929	London	Sonja Henie, Norway
1930	New York	Sonja Henie, Norway
1931	Berlin	Sonja Henie, Norway
1932	Montreal	Sonja Henie, Norway
1933	Zurich	Sonja Henie, Norway
1934	Stockholm	Sonja Henie, Norway
1935	Budapest	Sonja Henie, Norway
1936	Paris	Sonja Henie, Norway
1937	Vienna	Cecilia Colledge, Great Britain
1938	Berlin	Megan Taylor, Great Britain
1939	Budapest	Megan Taylor, Great Britain
1947	Stockholm	Barbara Ann Scott, Canada
1948	Davos	Barbara Ann Scott, Canada
1949	Paris	Alena Vrzanova, Czechoslovakia
1950	London	Alena Vrzanova, Czechoslovakia
1951	Milan	Jeanette Altwegg, Great Britain
1952	Paris	Jacqueline du Bief, France
1953	Davos	Tenley Albright, United States of America
1954	Oslo	Gundi Busch, West Germany
1955	Vienna	Tenley Albright, United States of America
1956	Garmisch	Carol Heiss, United States of America
1957	Colo Springs	Carol Heiss, United States of America
1958	Paris	Carol Heiss, United States of America
1959	Colo Springs	Carol Heiss, United States of America
1960	Vancouver	Carol Heiss, United States of America
1961	No championships held	
1962	Prague	Sjoukie Dijkstra, The Netherlands
1963	Cortina	Sjoukie Dijkstra, The Netherlands
1964	Dortmund	Sjoukie Dijkstra, The Netherlands
1965	Colo Springs	Petra Burka, Canada
1966	Davos	Peggy Fleming, United States of America
1967	Vienna	Peggy Fleming, United States of America
1968	Geneva	Peggy Fleming, United States of America
1969	Colo Springs	Gabriele Seyfert, East Germany
1970	Ljubjana	Gabriele Seyfert, East Germany
1971	Lyon	Beatrix Schuba, Austria
1972	Calgary	Beatrix Schuba, Austria
1973	Bratislava	Karen Magnussen, Canada
1974	Munich	Christine Errath, East Germany
1975	Colo Springs	Dianne de Leeuw, The Netherlands
1976	Gothenburg	Dorothy Hamill, United States of America
1977	Tokyo	Linda Fratianne, United States of America
1978	Ottawa	Anett Potzsch, East Germany
1979	Vienna	Linda Fratianne, United States of America
1980	Dortmund	Anett Potzsch, East Germany
1981	Hartford	Denise Biellmann, Switzerland
1982	Copenhagen	Elaine Zayak, United States of America
1983	Helsinki	Rosalyn Summers, United States of America
1984	Ottawa	Katarina Witt, East Germany
1985	Tokyo	Katarina Witt, East Germany
1986	Geneva	Debi Thomas, United States of America
1987	Cincinnati	Katarina Witt, East Germany
1988	Budapest	Katarina Witt, East Germany
1989	Paris	Midori Ito, Japan
1990	Halifax	Jill Trenary, United States of America
1991	Munich	Kristi Yamaguchi, United States of America
1992	Oakland	Kristi Yamaguchi, United States of America
1993	Prague	Oksana Baiul, Ukraine
1994	Chiba	Yuka Sato, Japan
1995	Birmingham	Chen Lu, China
1996	Edmonton	Michelle Kwan, United States of America
1997	Lausanne	Tara Lipinski, United States of America
1998	Minneapolis	Michelle Kwan, United States of America
1999	Helsinki	Maria Butyrskaya, Russia

PAIRS

1908	St Petersburg	Anna Hubler & Heinrich Burger, Germany
1909	Stockholm	Phyllis Johnson & James Johnson, Great Britain
1910	Davos	Anna Hubler & Heinrich Burger, Germany
1911	Berlin	Ludowika Eilers Germany & Walter Jakobsson, Finland
1912	Manchester	Phyllis Johnson & James Johnson, Great Britain
1913	Vienna	Helene Angelmann & Karl Mejstrik, Austria
1914	Helsinki	Ludowika Jakobsson & Walter Jakobsson, Finland
1922	Stockholm	Helene Engelmann & Alfred Berger, Austria
1923	Vienna	Ludowika Jakobsson & Walter Jakobsson, Finland
1924	Manchester	Helene Engelmann & Alfred Berger, Austria
1925	Vienna	Herma Jaross-Szabo & Ludwig Wrede, Austria
1926	Berlin	Andree Joly & Pierre Brunet, France
1927	Davos	Herma Jaross-Szabo & Ludwig Wrede, Austria
1928	Berlin	Andree Joly & Pierre Brunet, France
1929	London	Lily Scholz & Otto Kaiser, Austria
1930	New York	Andree Brunet & Pierre Brunet, France
1931	Berlin	Emilie Rotter & Lazlo Szollas, Hungary
1932	Montreal	Andree Brunet & Pierre Brunet, France

1933	Zurich	Emilie Rotter & Lazlo Szollas, Hungary
1934	Stockholm	Emilie Rotter & Lazlo Szollas, Hungary
1935	Budapest	Emilie Rotter & Lazlo Szollas, Hungary
1936	Paris	Maxi Herber & Ernst Baier, Germany
1937	Vienna	Maxi Herber & Ernst Baier, Germany
1938	Berlin	Maxi Herber & Ernst Baier, Germany
1939	Budapest	Maxi Herber & Ernst Baier, Germany
1947	Stockholm	Micheline Lannoy & Pierre Baugniet, Belgium
1948	Davos	Micheline Lannoy & Pierre Baugniet, Belgium
1949	Paris	Andrea Kekessy & Ede Kiraly, Hungary
1950	London	Karol Kennedy & Peter Kennedy, United States of America
1951	Milan	Ria Baran & Paul Falk, West Germany
1952	Paris	Ria Falk & Paul Falk, West Germany
1953	Davos	Jennifer Nicks & John Nicks, Great Britain
1954	Oslo	Frances Dafoe & Norris Bowden, Canada
1955	Vienna	Frances Dafoe & Norris Bowden, Canada
1956	Garmisch	Elisabeth Schwartz & Kurt Oppelt, Austria
1957	Colo Springs	Barbara Wagner & Robert Paul, Canada
1958	Paris	Barbara Wagner & Robert Paul, Canada
1959	Colo Springs	Barbara Wagner & Robert Paul, Canada
1960	Vancouver	Barbara Wagner & Robert Paul, Canada
1961		No championships held
1962	Prague	Maria Jelilnek & Otto Jelilnek, Canada
1963	Cortina	Marika Kilius & Hans Baumier, West Germany
1964	Dortmund	Marika Kilius & Hans Baumier, West Germany
1965	Colo Springs	Ludmila Belousova & Oleg Protopopov, Soviet Union
1966	Davos	Ludmila Belousova & Oleg Protopopov, Soviet Union
1967	Vienna	Ludmila Belousova & Oleg Protopopov, Soviet Union
1968	Geneva	Ludmila Belousova & Oleg Protopopov, Soviet Union
1969	Colo Springs	Irina Rodnina & Alexei Ulanov, Soviet Union
1970	Ljubjana	Irina Rodnina & Alexei Ulanov, Soviet Union
1971	Lyon	Irina Rodnina & Alexei Ulanov, Soviet Union
1972	Calgary	Irina Rodnina & Alexei Ulanov, Soviet Union
1973	Bratislava	Irina Rodnina & Alexei Ulanov, Soviet Union
1974	Munich	Irina Rodnina & Alexei Ulanov, Soviet Union
1975	Colo Springs	Irina Rodnina & Alexei Ulanov, Soviet Union
1976	Gothenburg	Irina Rodnina & Alexei Ulanov, Soviet Union

1977	Tokyo	Irina Rodnina & Alexei Ulanov, Soviet Union
1978	Ottawa	Irina Rodnina & Alexei Ulanov, Soviet Union
1979	Vienna	Tai Babilonia & Randy Gardner, United States of America
1980	Dortmund	Marina Cherkasova & Sergei Shakhrai, Soviet Union
1981	Hartford	Irina Vorobieva & Igor Lisovsky, Soviet Union
1982	Copenhagen	Sabine Baess & Tassilo Thierbach, East Germany
1983	Helsinki	Elena Valova & Oleg Vasiliev, Soviet Union
1984	Ottawa	Barbara Underhill & Paul Martini, Canada
1985	Tokyo	Elena Valova & Oleg Vasiliev, Soviet Union
1986	Geneva	Ekaterina Gordeeva & Sergei Grinkov, Soviet Union
1987	Cincinnati	Ekaterina Gordeeva & Sergei Grinkov, Soviet Union
1988	Budapest	Elena Valova & Oleg Vasiliev, Soviet Union
1989	Paris	Ekaterina Gordeeva & Sergei Grinkov, Soviet Union
1990	Halifax	Ekaterina Gordeeva & Sergei Grinkov, Soviet Union
1991	Munich	Natalia Mishkutenok & Artur Dmitriev, Soviet Union
1992	Oakland	Natalia Mishkutenok & Artur Dmitriev, Soviet Union
1993	Prague	Isabelle Brasseur & Lloyd Eisler, Canada
1994	Chiba	Evgenia Shishkova & Vadim Naumov, Russia
1995	Birmingham	Radka Kovarikova & Rene Novotny, Czech Republic
1996	Edmonton	Marina Eltsova & Andrei Bushkov, Russia
1997	Lausanne	Mandy Wotzel & Ingo Steur, Germany
1998	Minneapolis	Elena Berezhnaya & Anton Sikharulidze, Russia
1999	Helsinki	Elena Berezhnaya & Anton Sikharulidze, Russia

ICE DANCING

1952	Paris	Jean Westwood & Lawrence Demmy, Great Britain
1953	Davos	Jean Westwood & Lawrence Demmy, Great Britain
1954	Oslo	Jean Westwood & Lawrence Demmy, Great Britain
1955	Vienna	Jean Westwood & Lawrence Demmy, Great Britain
1956	Garmisch	Pamela Weight & Paul Thomas, Great Britain
1957	Colo Springs	June Markham & Courtney Jones, Great Britain
1958	Paris	June Markham & Courtney Jones, Great Britain
1959	Colo Springs	Doreen Denny & Courtney Jones, Great Britain
1960	Vancouver	Doreen Denny & Courtney Jones, Great Britain
1961		No championships held
1961	Prague	Eva Romanova & Pavel Roman, Czechoslovakia
1963	Cortina	Eva Romanova & Pavel Roman, Czechoslovakia

1964	Dortmund	Eva Romanova & Pavel Roman, Czechoslovakia
1965	Colo Springs	Eva Romanova & Pavel Roman, Czechoslovakia
1966	Davos	Diane Towler & Bernard Ford, Great Britain
1967	Vienna	Diane Towler & Bernard Ford, Great Britain
1968	Geneva	Diane Towler & Bernard Ford, Great Britain
1969	Colo Springs	Diane Towler & Bernard Ford, Great Britain
1970	Ljubljana	Liudmila Pakhomova & Alexandr Gorshkov, Soviet Union
1971	Lyon	Liudmila Pakhomova & Alexandr Gorshkov, Soviet Union
1972	Calgary	Liudmila Pakhomova & Alexandr Gorshkov, Soviet Union
1973	Bratislava	Liudmila Pakhomova & Alexandr Gorshkov, Soviet Union
1974	Munich	Liudmila Pakhomova & Alexandr Gorshkov, Soviet Union
1975	Colo Springs	Irina Moiseev & Andrei Minenko, Soviet Union
1976	Gothenburg	Liudmila Pakhomova & Alexandr Gorshkov, Soviet Union
1977	Tokyo	Irina Moiseeva & Andrei Minenkov, Soviet Union
1978	Ottawa	Natalia Linichuk & Gennadi Karponosov, Soviet Union
1979	Vienna	Natalia Linichuk & Gennadi Karponosov, Soviet Union
1980	Dortmund	Krisztine Regoeczy & Andras Sallay, Hungary
1981	Hartford	Jayne Torvill & Christopher Dean, Great Britain
1982	Copenhagen	Jayne Torvill & Christopher Dean, Great Britain
1983	Helsinki	Jayne Torvill & Christopher Dean, Great Britain
1984	Ottawa	Jayne Torvill & Christopher Dean, Great Britain
1985	Tokyo	Natalia Bestemianova & Andrei Bukin, Soviet Union
1986	Geneva	Natalia Bestemianova & Andrei Bukin, Soviet Union
1987	Cincinnati	Natalia Bestemianova & Andrei Bukin, Soviet Union
1988	Budapest	Natalia Bestemianova & Andrei Bukin, Soviet Union
1989	Paris	Marina Klimova & Sergei Ponomarenko, Soviet Union
1990	Halifax	Marina Klimova & Sergei Ponomarenko, Soviet Union
1991	Munich	Isabelle Duchesnay & Paul Duchesnay, France
1992	Oakland	Marina Klimova & Sergei Ponomarenko, Unified Team
1993	Prague	Usova & Zhulin, Russia
1994	Chiba	Oksana Grishuk & Evgeny Platov, Russia
1995	Birmingham	Oksana Grishuk & Evgeny Platov, Russia
1996	Edmonton	Oksana Grishuk & Evgeny Platov, Russia
1997	Lausanne	Oksana Grishuk & Evgeny Platov, Russia
1998	Minneapolis	Anjelika Krylova & Oleg Ovsyannikov, Russia
1999	Helsinki	Anjelika Krylova & Oleg Ovsyannikov, Russia